Waverly Honor

A workbook of Embroidery Design

with an appendix of whitework
embroidery instructions

Martha Anne Hart
& Hester Neblett

edited by Mary-Dick Digges
and illustrated by Jay Wortham

Embroidery Research Press, Inc.
Roswell, GA

Embroidery Research Press, Inc., Roswell, GA
©1989 by Embroidery Research Press, Inc. All rights reserved
Printed in the United States of America.

Library of Congress Cataloging in Publication Data
Hart, Martha Anne, 1926 -
    Waverly Honor: a workbook of embroidery design.
    Includes bibliographical references.
    1. Embroidery—Patterns.   2. White work embroidery—
Patterns. I. Neblett, Hester, 1910—   II. Digges
Mary—Dick, 1934—   III. Title.
    TT771.H232 1989   746.44′041   89-23677
ISBN 0-929339-02-9

Design and Art Direction: indelible inc./David Skinner and
Margaret Silver

Dedication

This book is dedicated to the memory of Virginia Baskervill, who had the foresight to record these needlework designs for the pleasure of future generations. The authors wish to thank Mrs. E. Hatcher Crenshaw, Jr., for allowing her portrait of Virginia Baskervill to be photographed for inclusion in this book. We are also grateful to Laura Anderson for her careful proofreading and to Nuncia Henneman for her research assistance at the Library of Congress. Finally, we wish to thank Margaret Lunt and Rosemary Cornelius for their advice on the whitework instructions which are given in the appendix.

Contents

Introduction

Wensley House

The designs in this book are taken from two notebooks, dated 1858, which were found in an old trunk in an attic. The notebooks belonged to Virginia Baskervill, who lived at Waverly Honor plantation in Mecklenburg County, Virginia. Miss Baskervill was the great-aunt of Sterling Neblett, whose wife, Hester, encouraged me to compile this book to share them with other needlewomen.

Many of the designs were copied from patterns of the day or from needlework at hand, and others are quite artistic in their free-flowing style. I have tried to reproduce them, as nearly as possible, in the manner in which they appear in the notebooks. They are not in the original order, as I felt they would be more useful if grouped into categories, for example, floral sprays, grape designs, borders, and so on.

There has been a great resurgence of interest in the needle arts in the past few years. I have become aware of this through my association with the Virginia Guild of Needlewomen. Among the techniques being revived are bobbin lace, needlelace, needlepoint, and many types of whitework, such as broderie anglaise, Madeira, Irishwork, drawnwork, and pulled thread, to name but a few. Many of the motifs that were used have held up well through the years.

The majority of designs presented here seem most appropriate for whitework, that is, white thread embroidery on white linen, cambric, or even a fine quality of muslin, depending on the use of the finished article. Some of the stitches used in whitework are satin stitch, flat, raised, or padded, French knots, point de pois or dot stitch, overcast edges, buttonhole edges and eyelets, back stitch, and rope stitch.

Other designs were found in shaded cotton or silk floss. Here the flat satin stitch and split satin stitch (long and short) were employed, with delicate shadings which produced the most beautiful results, the effect of which was equivalent to painting. Wool threads were used on linen in crewel embroidery in much the same way, with an even greater variety of stitches than mentioned before.

Note: All embroideries shown are the work of Virginia Baskervill.

Many times eyelets were employed in cutwork patterns and were used in conjunction with padded dots of all sizes. They were also used to embellish monograms, which were very popular in the 1800's. It may further be noted that the use of floral designs is found in Honiton lace.

Every household, however modest, had at least a few pieces of fine embroidery. Quite often needlework provided a livelihood for the women of the day. Estates and plantations had seamstresses and needlewomen as part of the household. It was their responsibility to keep the table linens, bed linens, and clothing in good order. We remember the many flounces and edgings on petticoats, sleeves, bodices, collars, and cuffs.

What a blessing it is that the art of needlework will not die, that attics still have old trunks, and that there will always be needlewomen who care enough to not allow themselves to be replaced by machines!

Martha Anne Hart
September, 1989

4

A Brief History

Accounts vary, but it is certain that the property on which Waverly Honor was to be constructed was acquired by the first Baskervill sometime in the third quarter of the eighteenth century. Family history says that this was Robert Baskervill, in 1752, and that in due course both house and property passed to his son William Baskervill, and to William's son, William Rust Baskervill. William Rust Baskervill and his wife, Sallie Dortch, had two children, Robert Dortch Baskervill and Virginia Baskervill, fondly known as Cousin Jennie. In 1856 Robert Dortch Baskervill, who had by then attended the University of Virginia and the University of Pennsylvania Medical School, married Bettye Park Alexander. Their daughter, Sallye T. Baskervill, married Clem Green Neblett, and they had a son, Sterling Neblett, who married Hester Deel. It was to Sterling Neblett that the notebooks and embroideries of Virginia Baskervill descended.

In 1935 the Works Progress Administration (known as the WPA) was established by the federal government. Among its aims was the provision of work for the unemployed by means of grants to individual states. One of the WPA projects undertaken in Virginia was the cataloging of houses of historical interest, of which Waverly Honor was one. According to their report the land was purchased by George Baskerville from Peter Fields Jefferson in 1760, and the house was built about 1769.*

It was located one-and-a-quarter miles southeast of Red Lawn, Virginia, three-tenths of a mile south of what is now State Route 637. The WPA records that the property passed to John Baskerville in 1777, and to Col. William R. Baskerville in 1779. It remained in family hands until its purchase in 1893 by William Morton. The description, which was written in 1937, relates the following:

> This house was a real mansion in its day, with its flower garden and sunken garden, beautiful yard, flower houses

* WPA records differ from family usage in the adding of an e to the spelling of Baskervill.

and a handsome office where the landlord issued orders to his three hundred slaves. The office has its round colonial columns, high ceiling, high windows, beautifully plastered walls and open fireplaces.

The flower garden still has shrubs of every kind and size, many bulbs, grape vines, and box trees eighteen feet high, beautiful in shape and foliage. Shrubs and crape myrtles have grown to be real trees around the edges of the sunken garden. Magnolia trees are in the front yard, and on each side of the walk from the house to the yard gate are box-bushes. Across the front yard and out in the front lawn is Scotch Broom.

On the left side of the yard stand two brick flower houses, plastered on the inside and finished just as a room of the dwelling house. The brick used in these flower houses were taken from the place where Fields Jefferson built the first house on this land before selling it to the Baskervilles.

The front porch has quite a lot of fancy carving between the columns, and fancy transoms over the large double doors and side transoms that form the entrance to the long hall that runs across the front from the north to the south wing.

The south wing was the parlor, and a very large room with paper on the walls that was said to have been put on it at the time of building. The north wing was the mistress's bedroom. Each of these rooms has an open fireplace that has arches made of three pieces of marble, and the mantels are low and prettily carved but not fancy.

All of these rooms have wainscoting that is twenty-seven inches wide, extending the length of the rooms, without a single knot or blemish in the wood. In one room at the front the wainscoting is hand carved in a fish design, and in another the design is known as the curtain. The maids' rooms on the third floor are the only rooms that have no fireplaces.

There is a quaint flight of steps in the rear hall that leads to the second floor of the oldest part of this house. These steps are small and narrow and are painted to represent marble.

The timbers for this home were sawed with a whipsaw pulled by slave labor, and wooden pegs and shop nails were used in the construction. The basement affords large storage quarters and a nice wine cellar.

The architectural survey of the house further states that it was a frame, T-shaped, two-story structure (plus cellar and attic), with fourteen rooms, six chimneys, and a metal roof. As points of historical significance it states that the patriarch of the family was George Baskerville, who emigrated from England, living first in Surry County, Virginia, and that it was his first son, John, who inherited the estate from him in 1777. Two years later it passed to William Rust Baskerville, who was the father of Virginia Baskerville.

The story is told that Virginia Baskervill was in love with a young man who went off to fight in the War Between the States and never returned. Perhaps she busied herself with needlework to keep from dwelling on her loss. Her lovely home, Waverly Honor, is no longer standing, but the elegance of that bygone era lives on in the designs she lovingly collected.

Designs

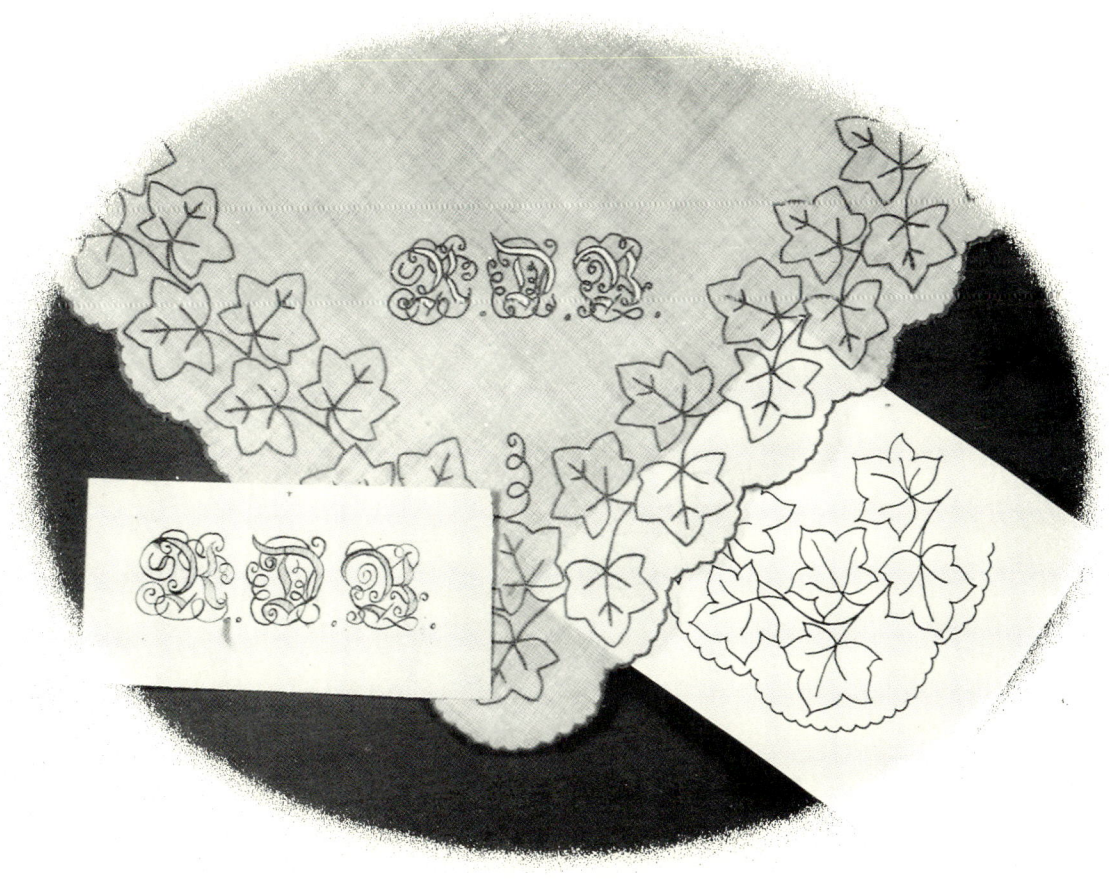

Floral Units

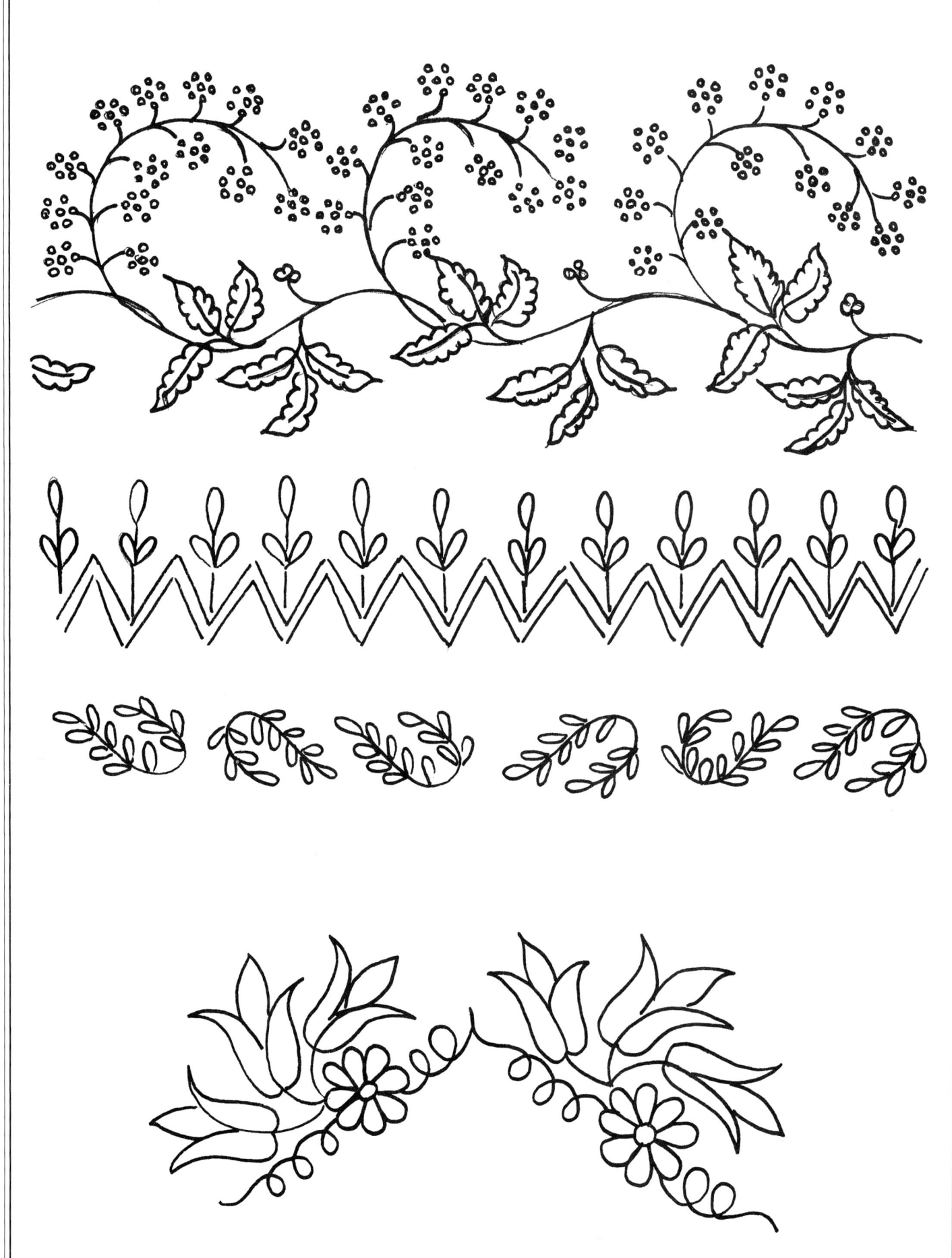

each box = 1 inch

each box = 1 inch

Borders

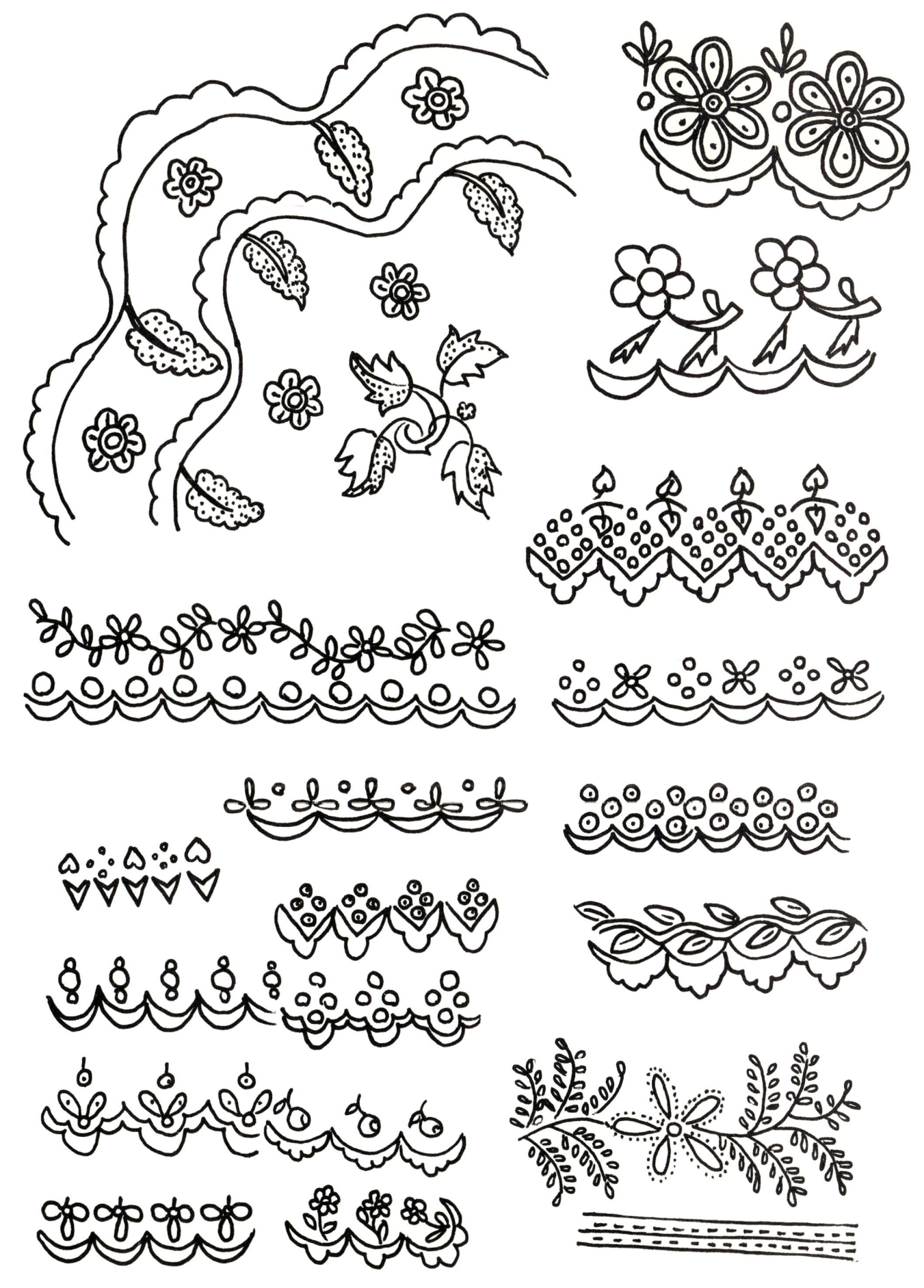

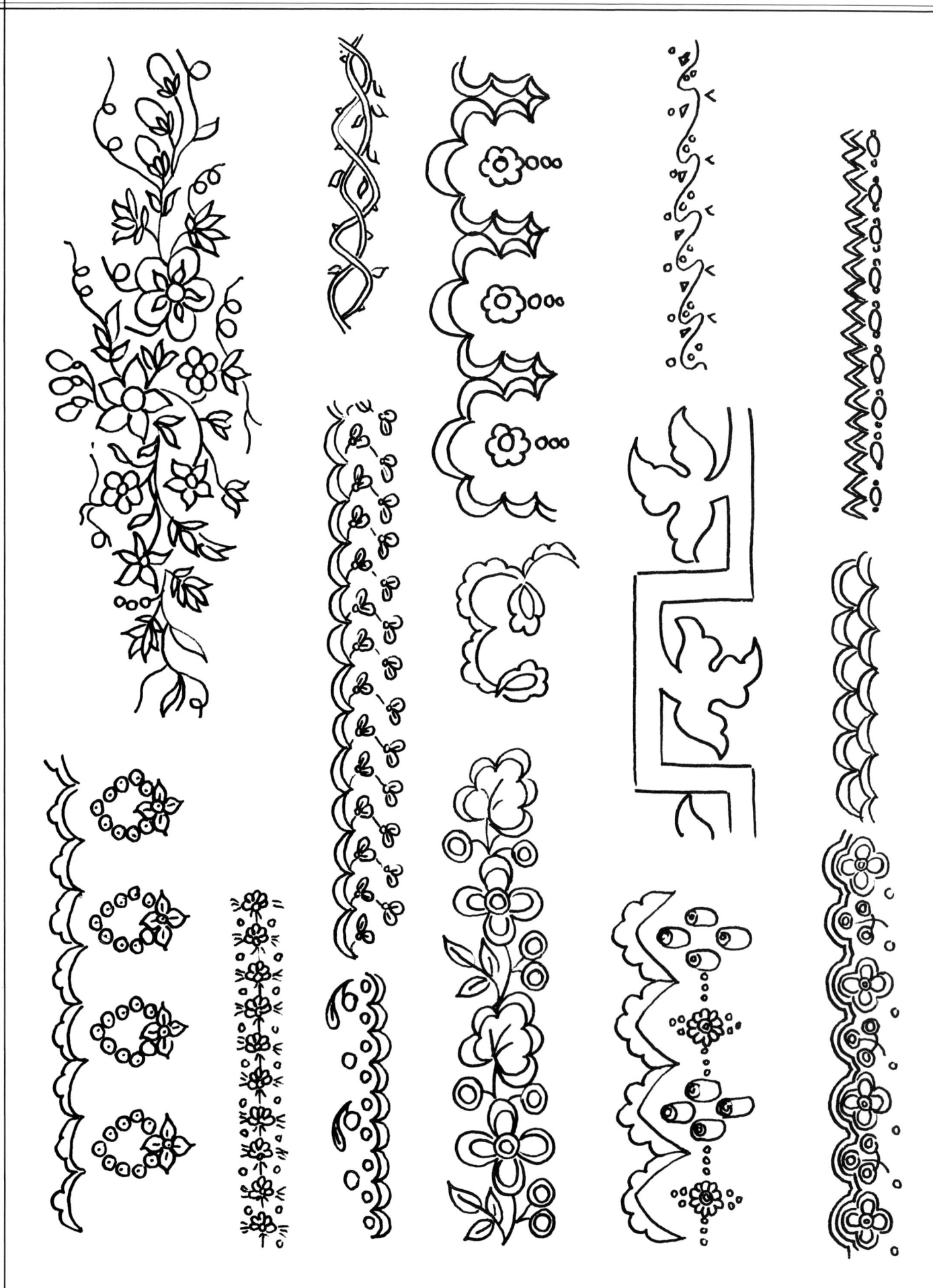

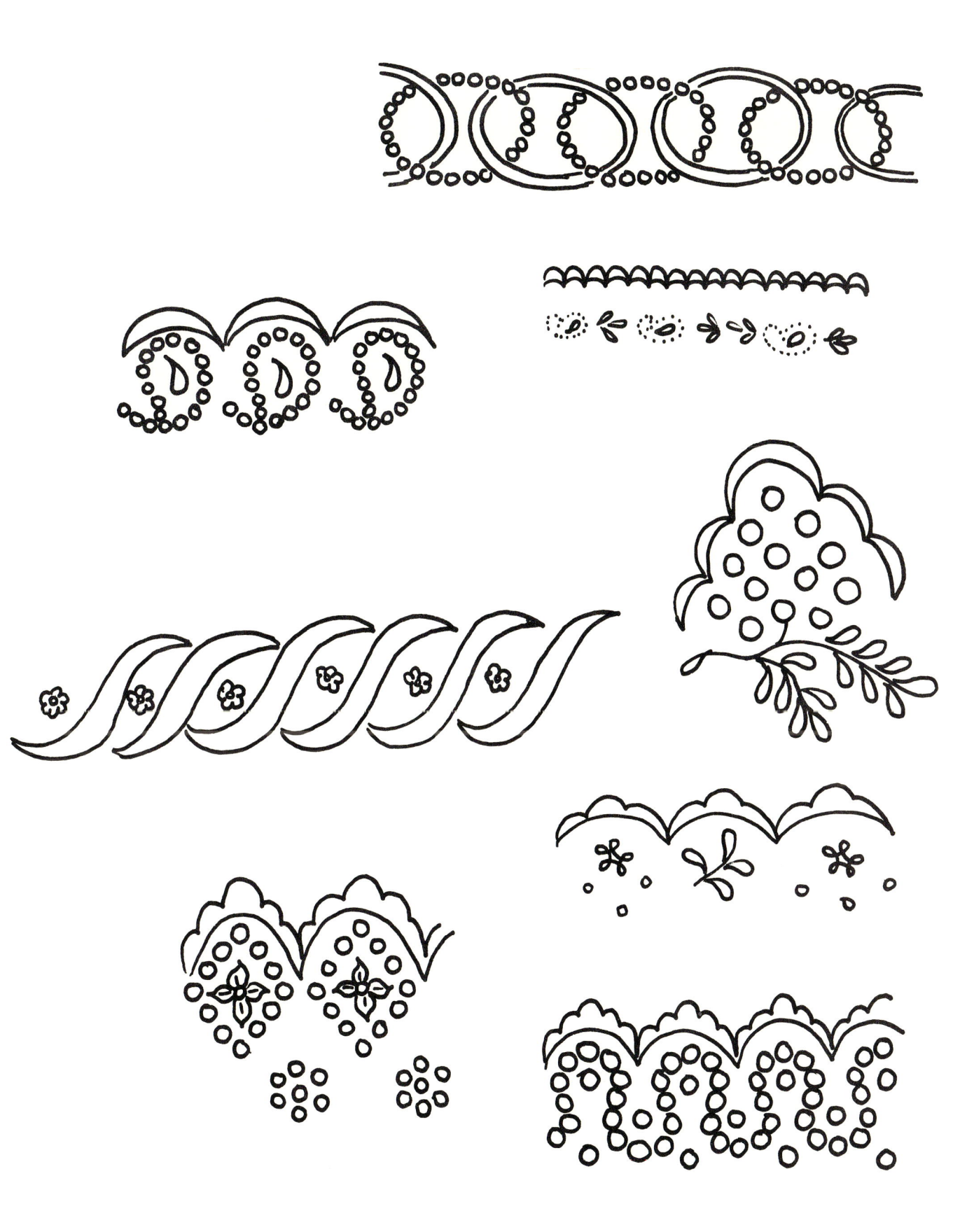

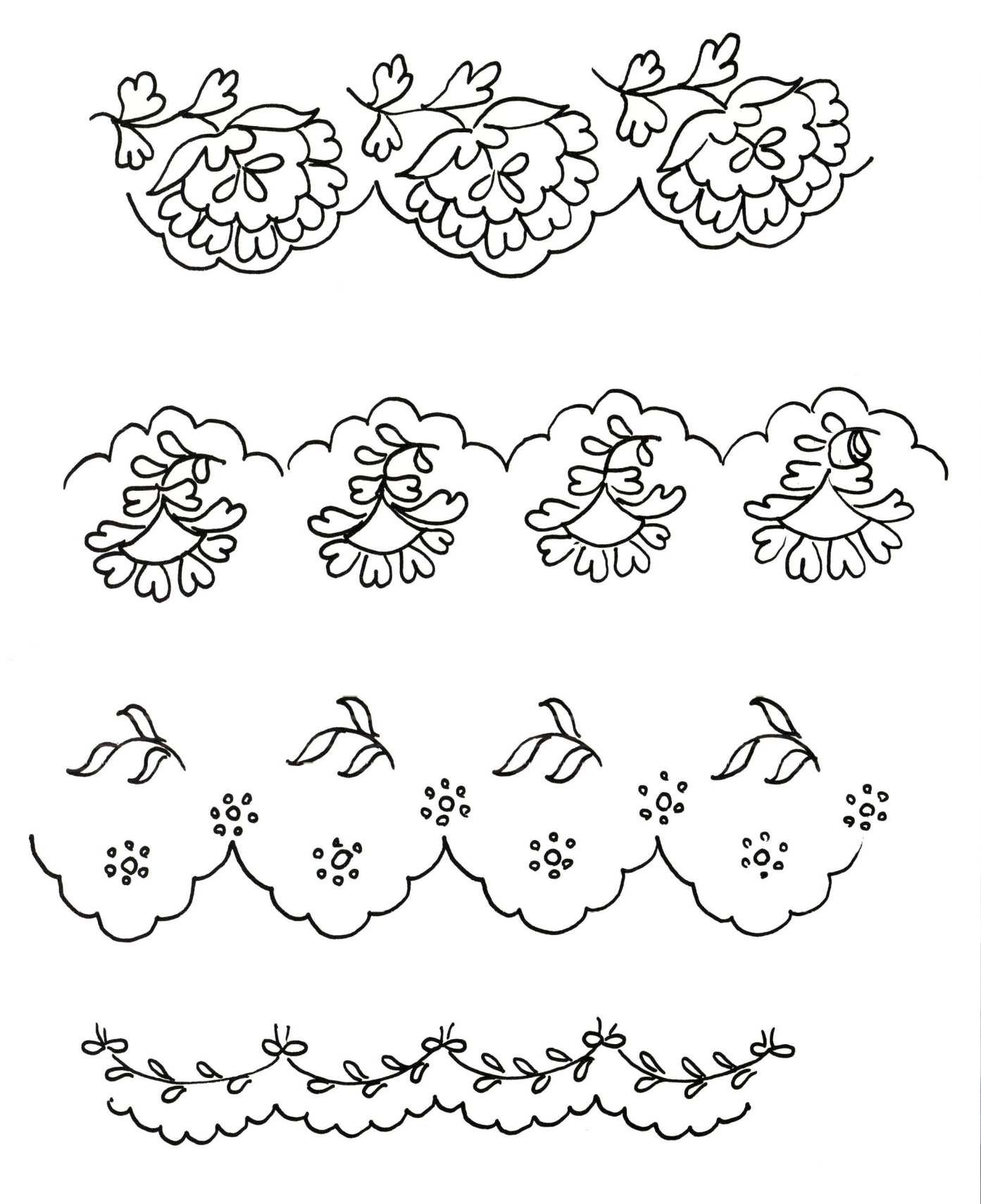

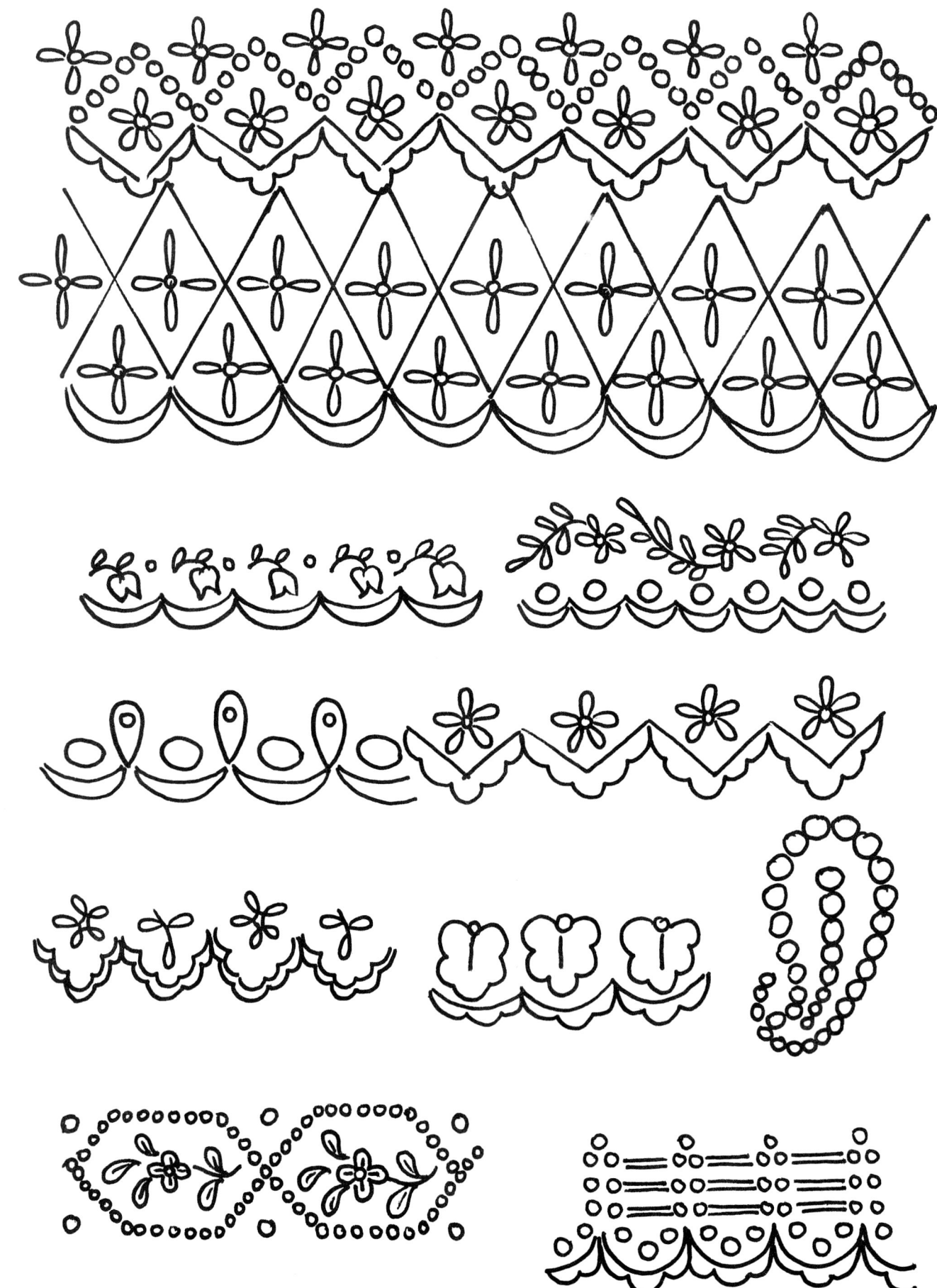

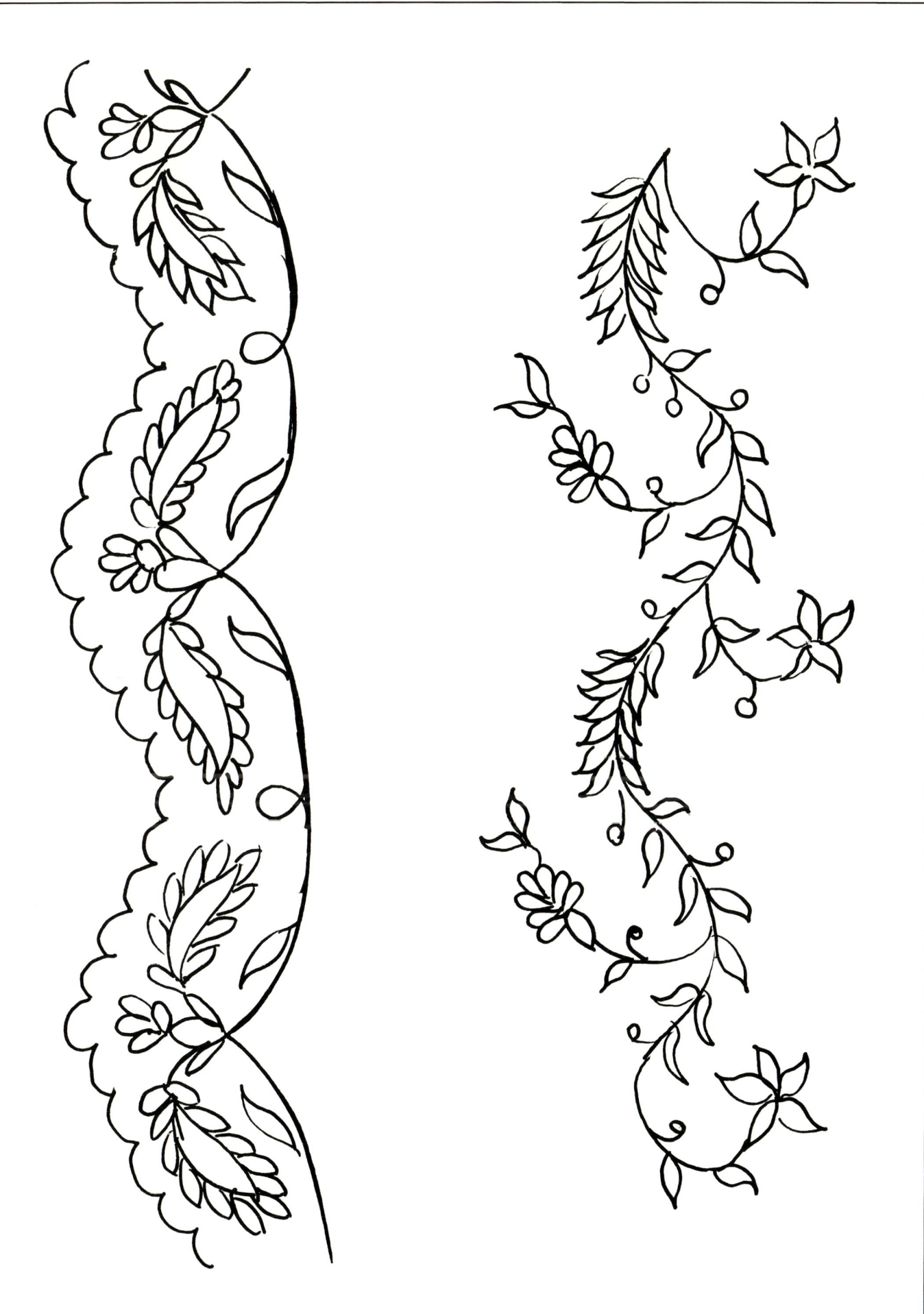

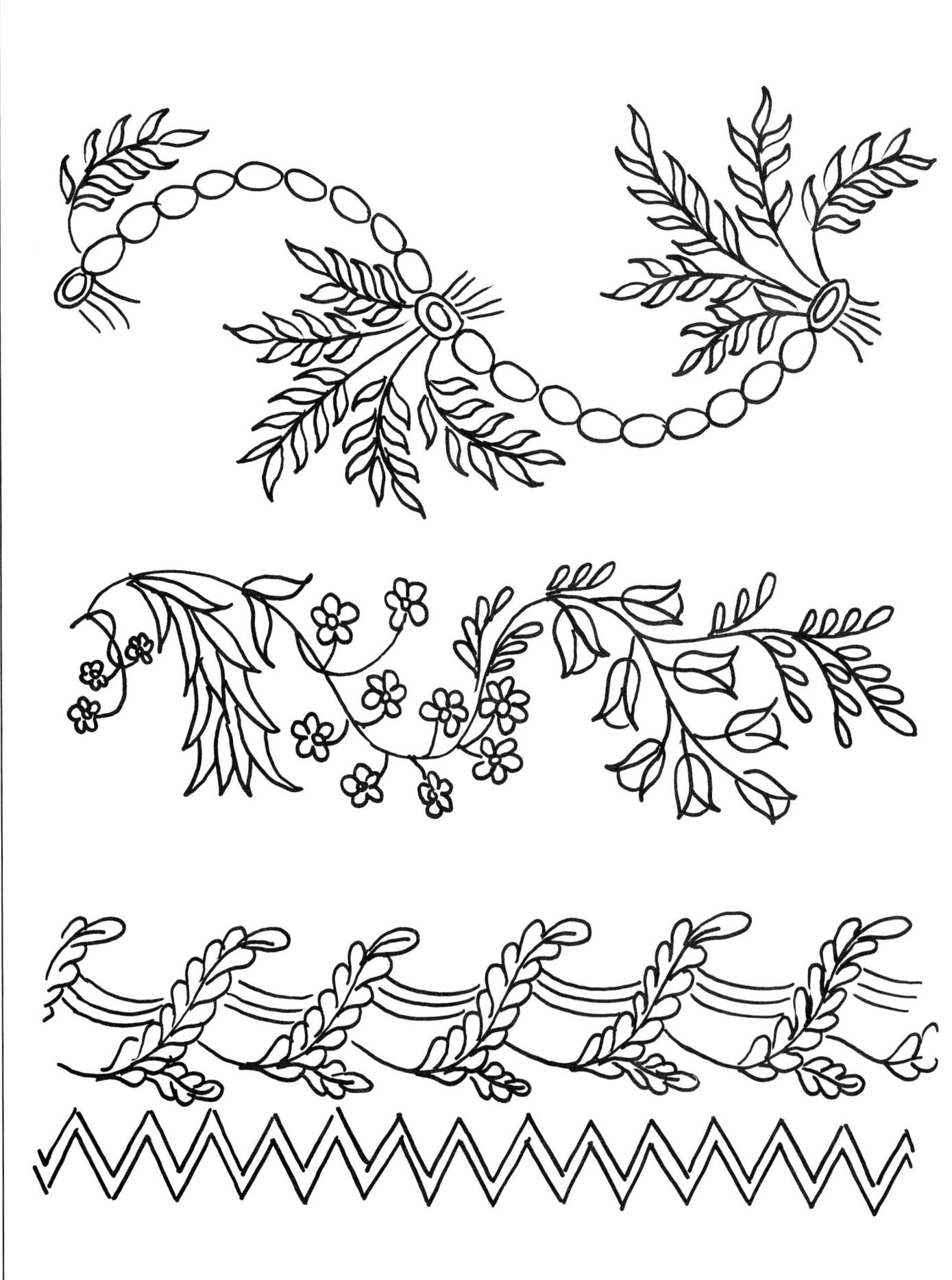

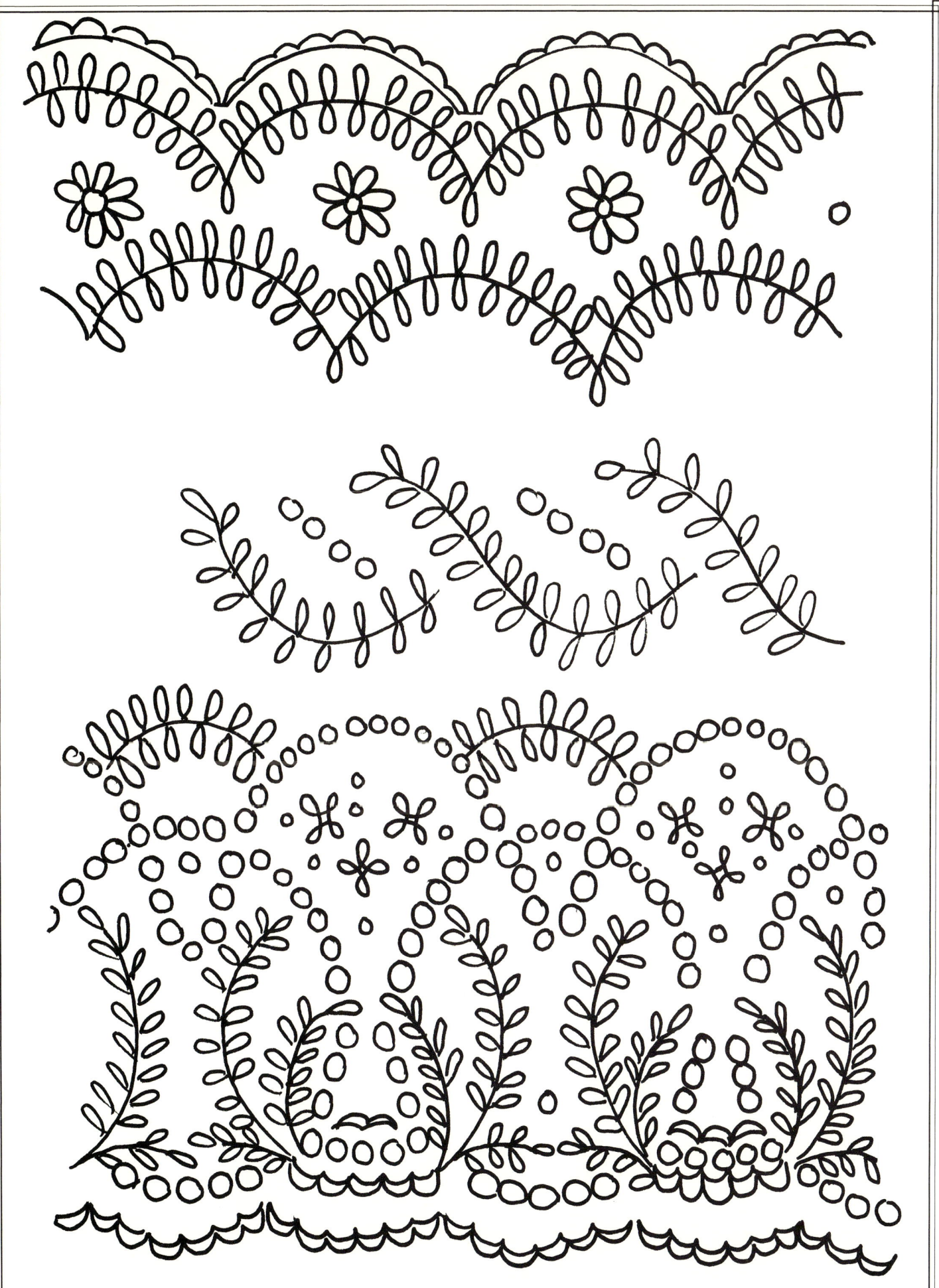

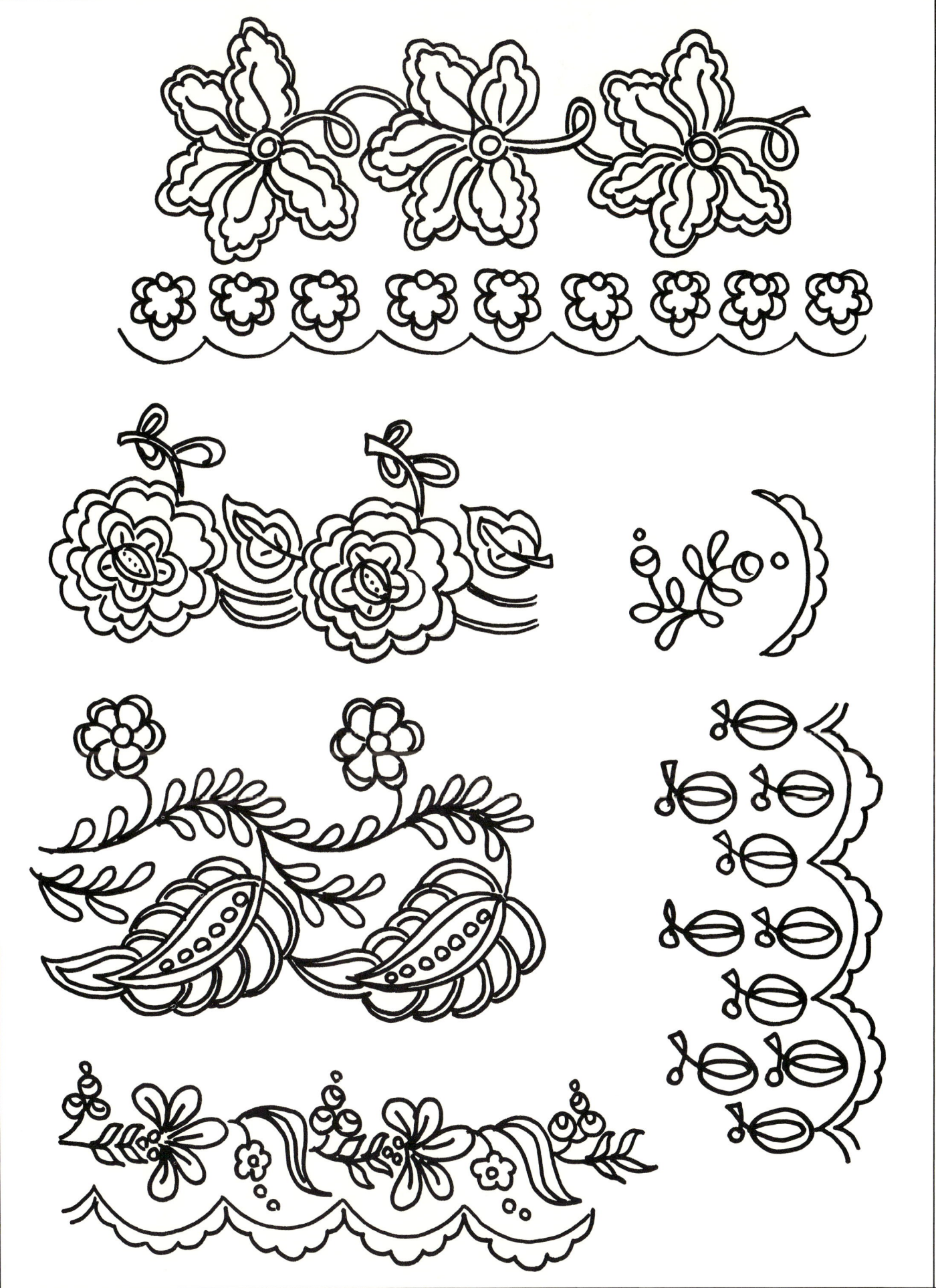

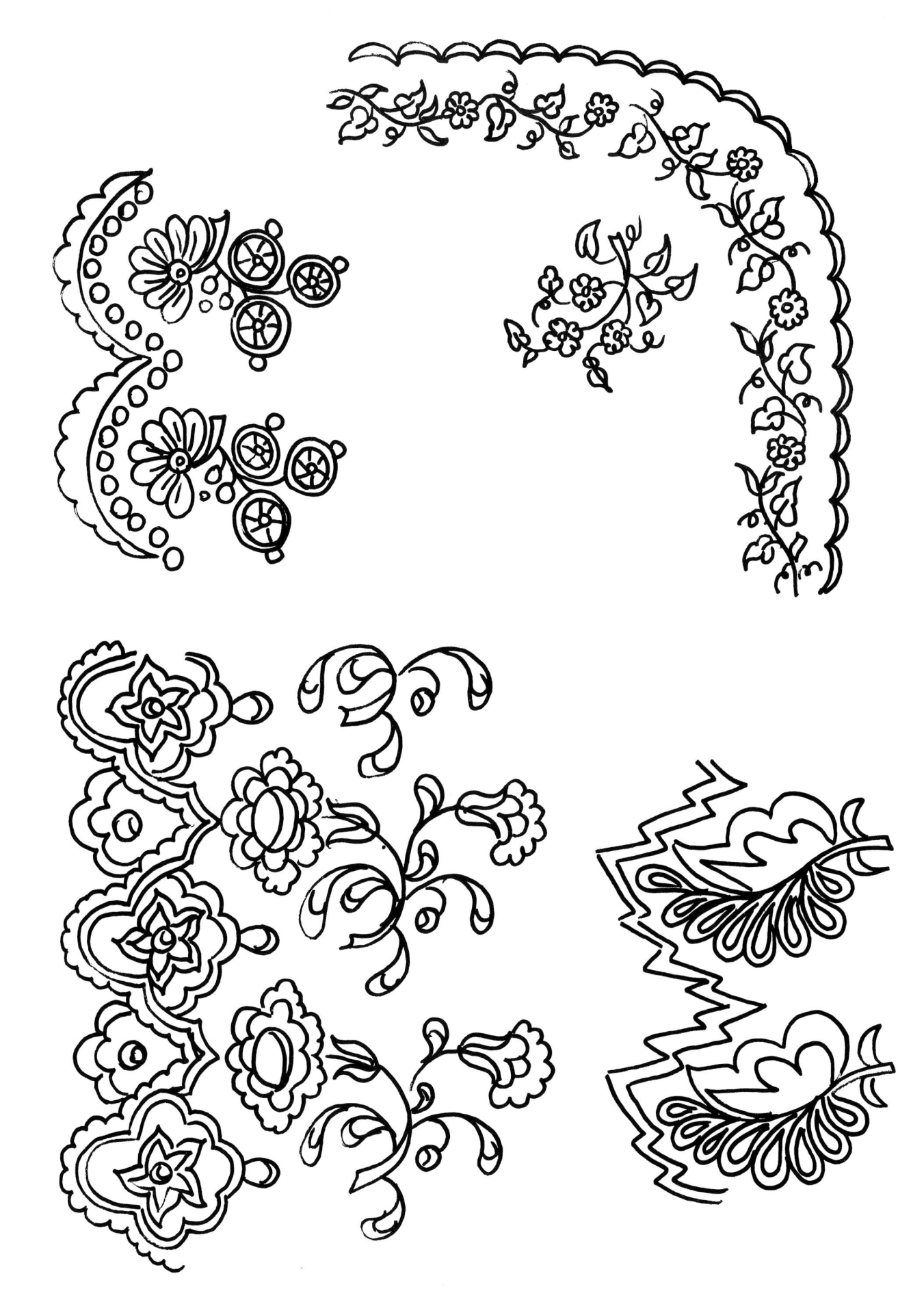

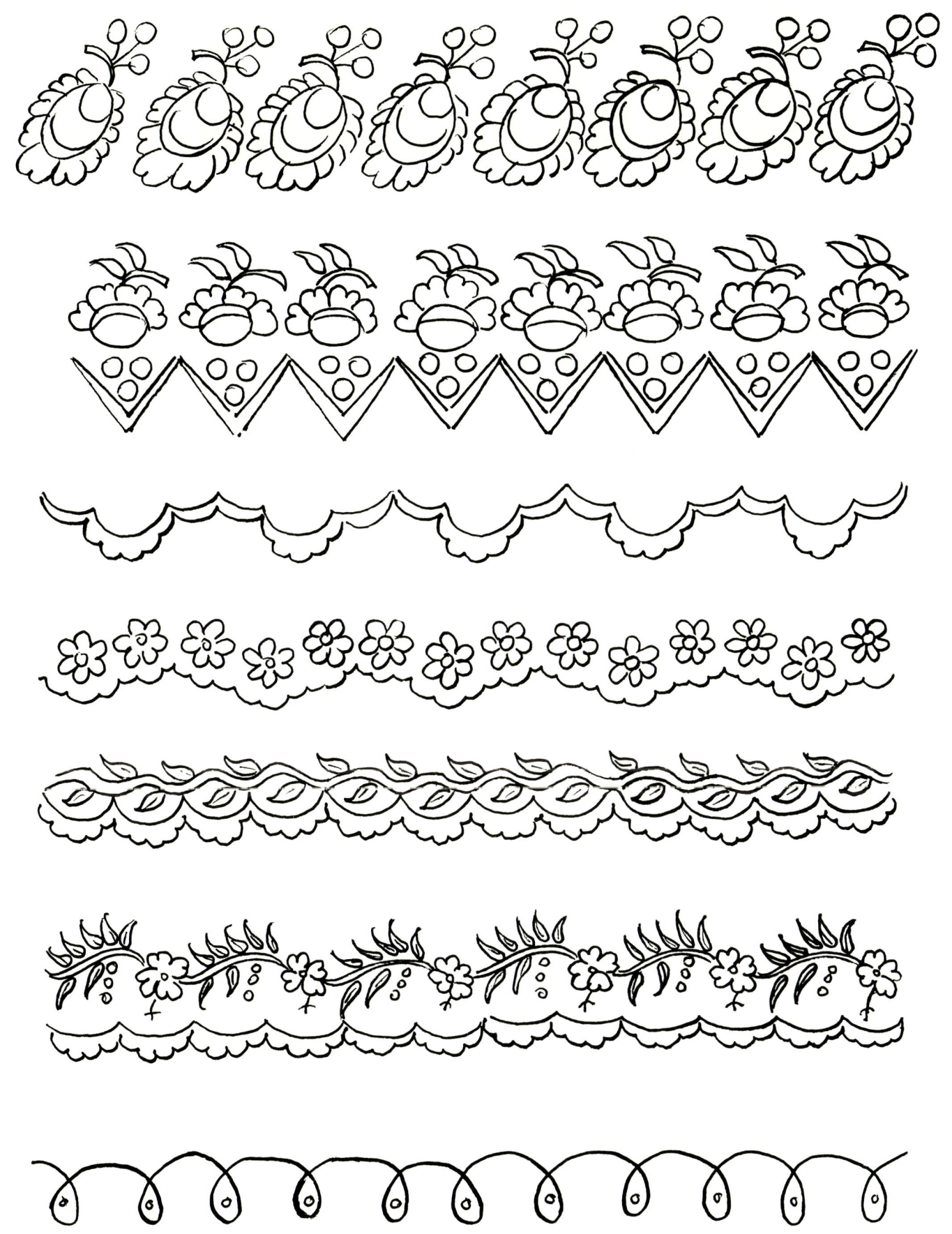

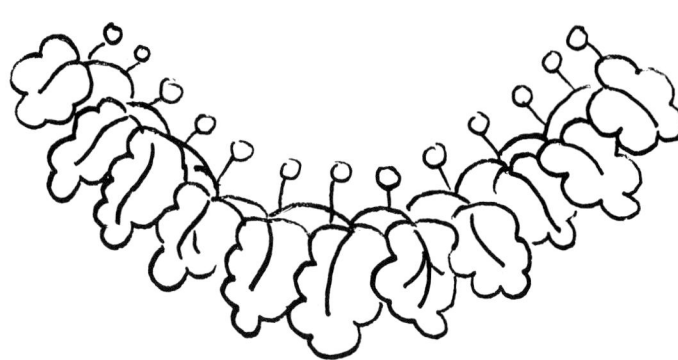

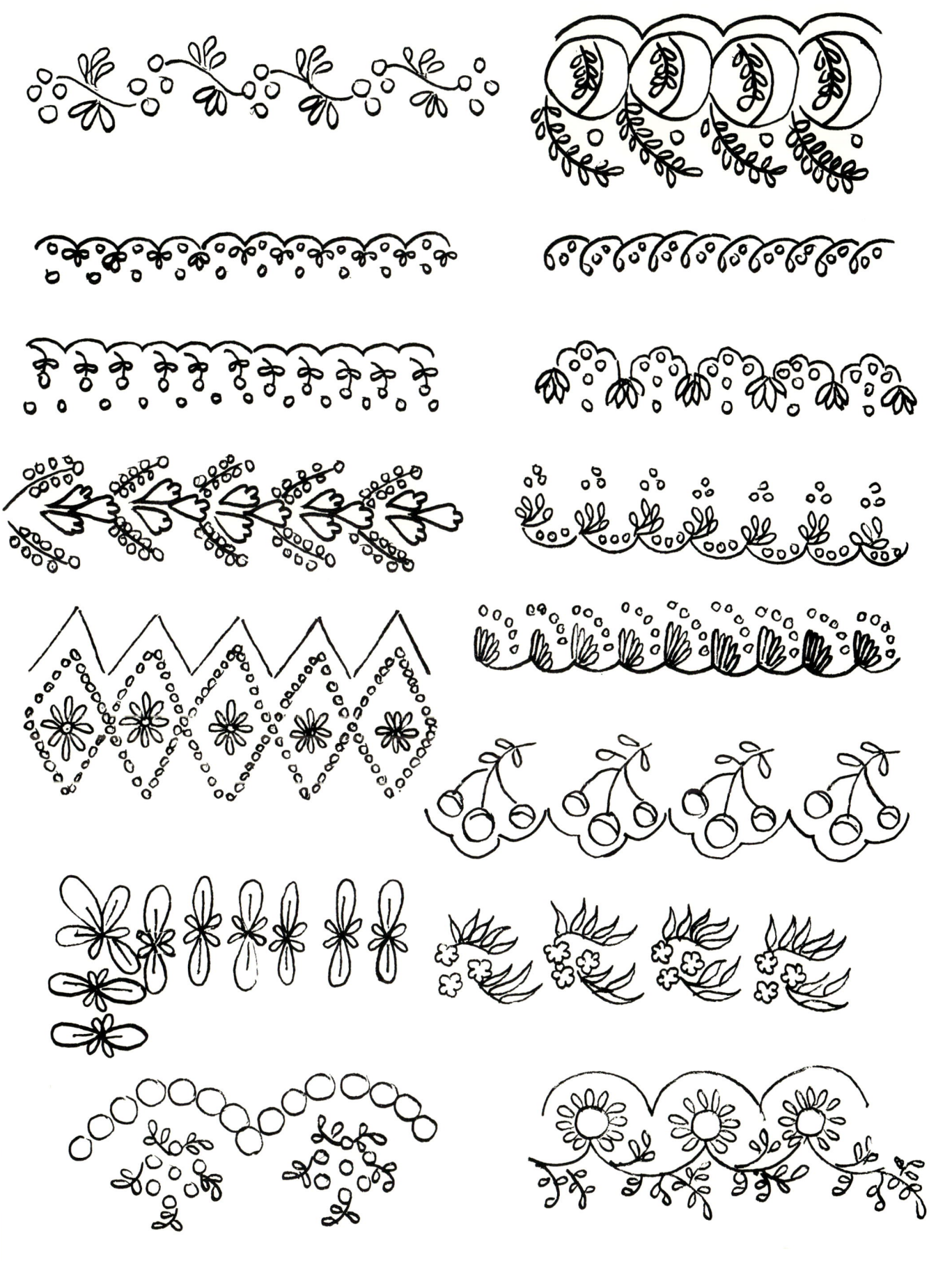

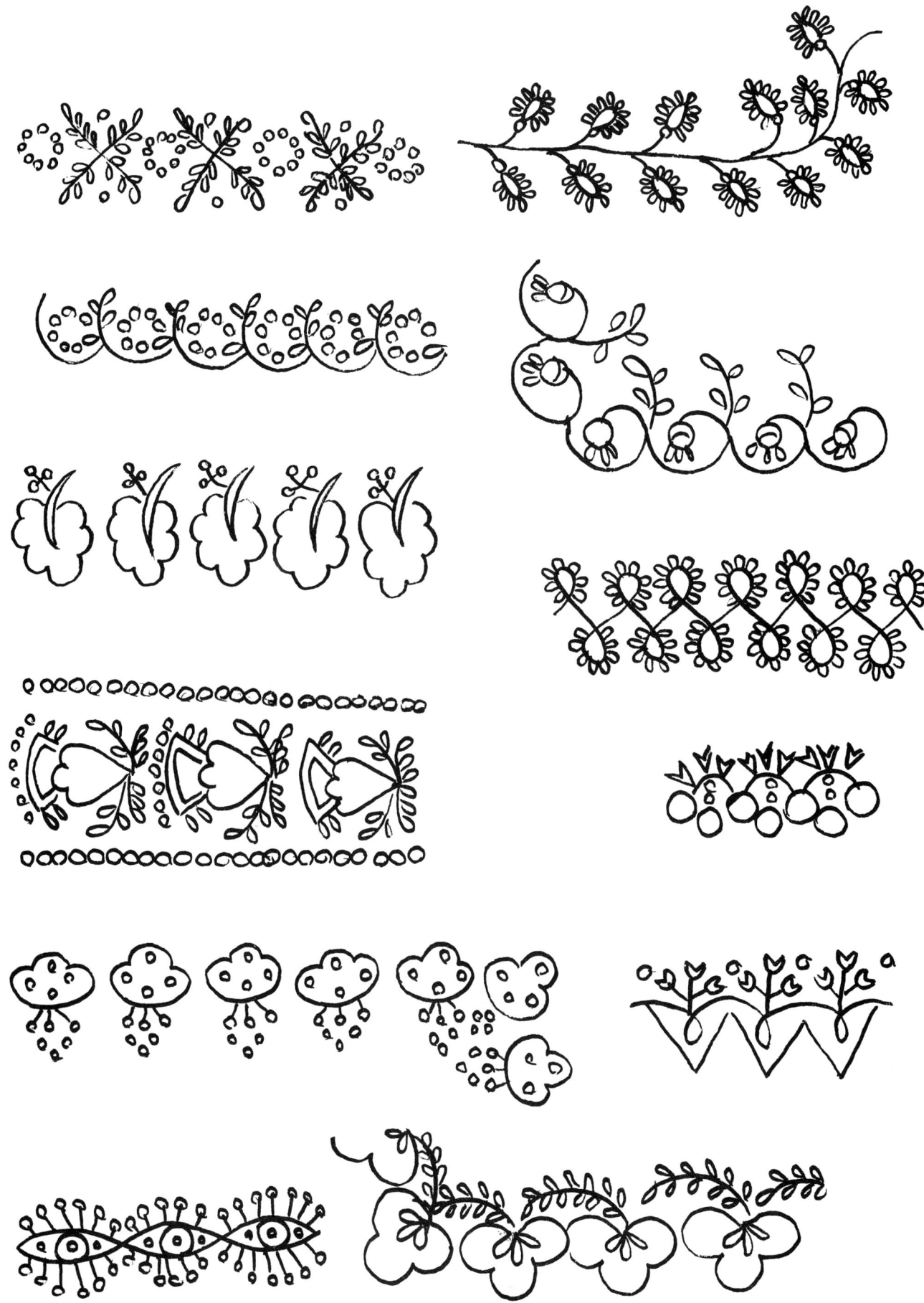

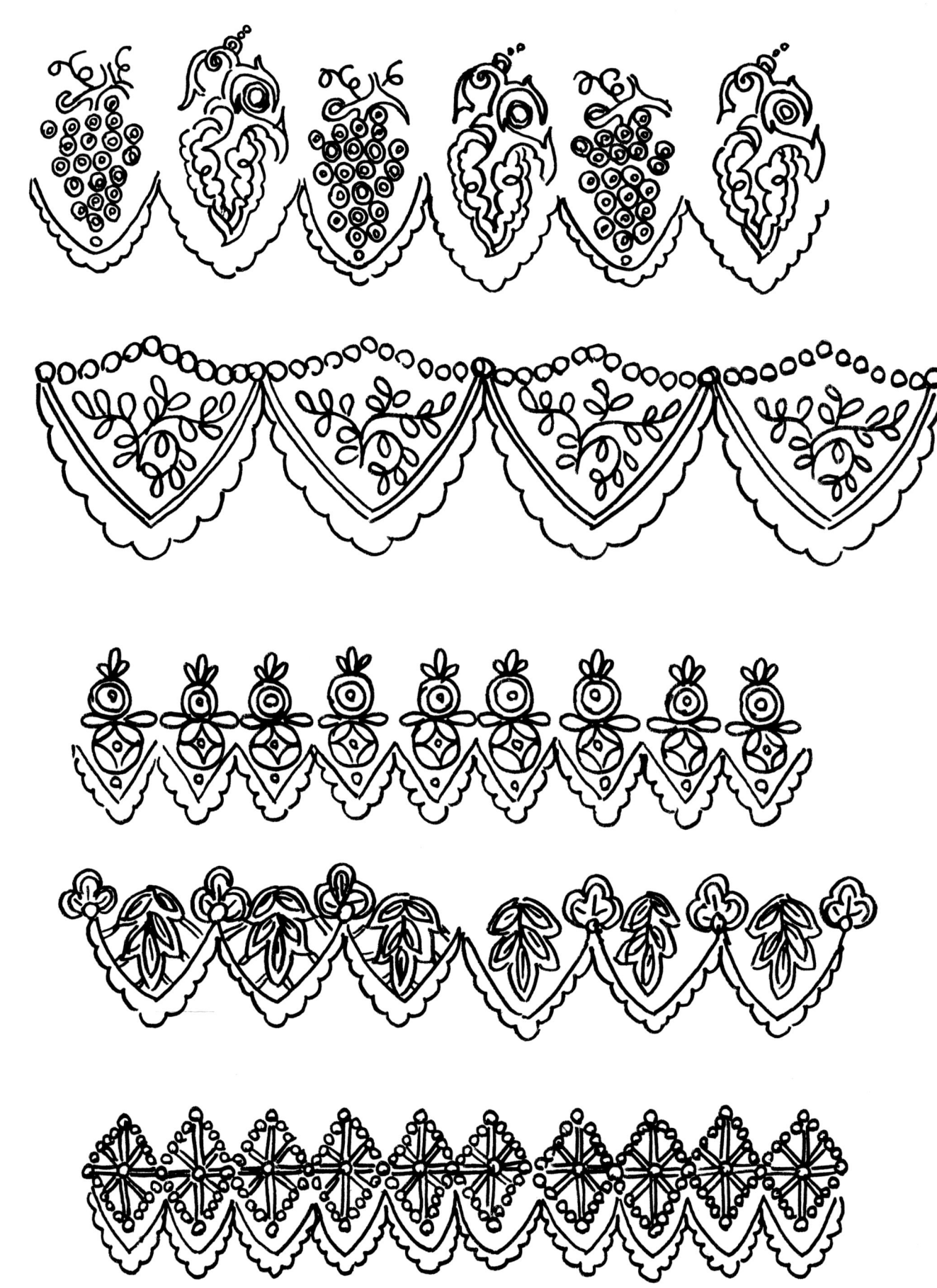

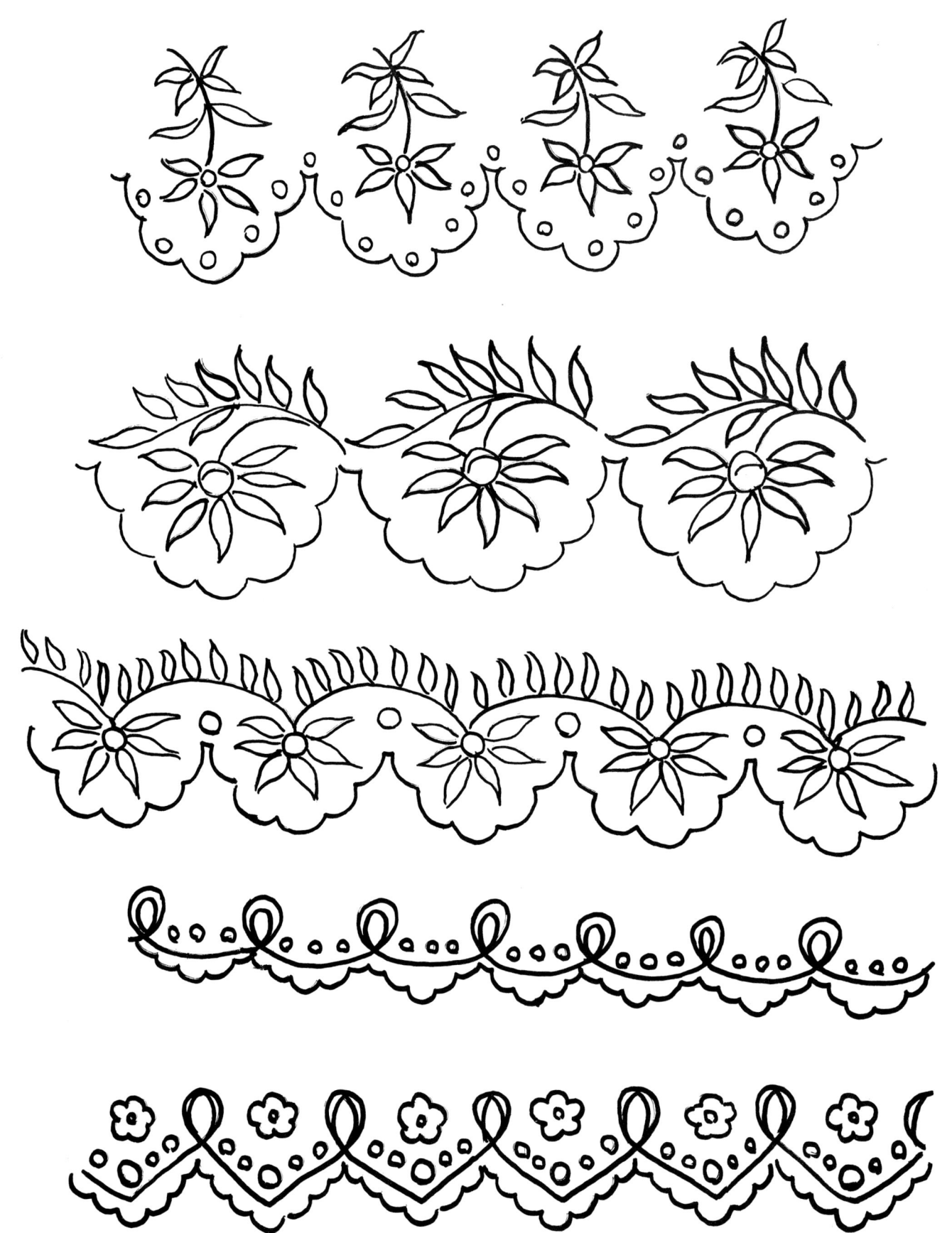

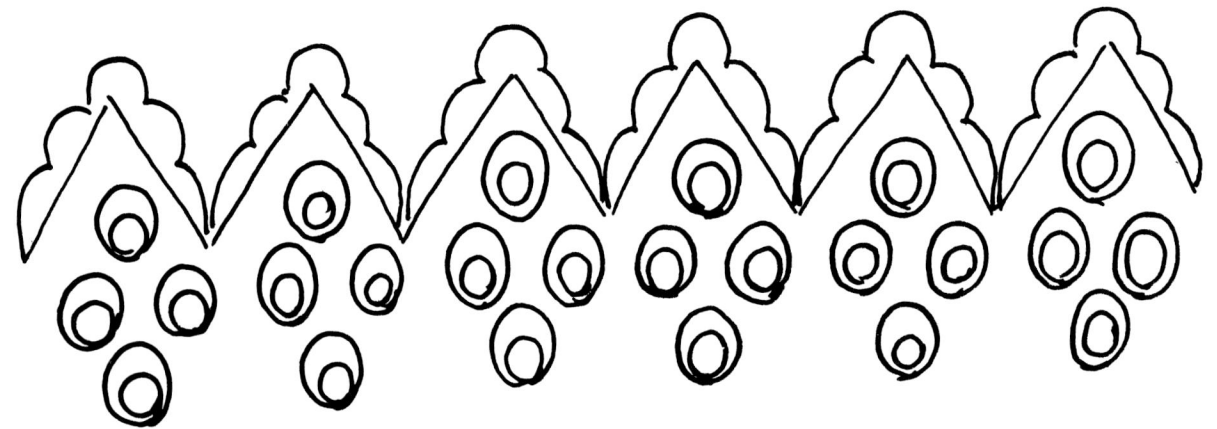

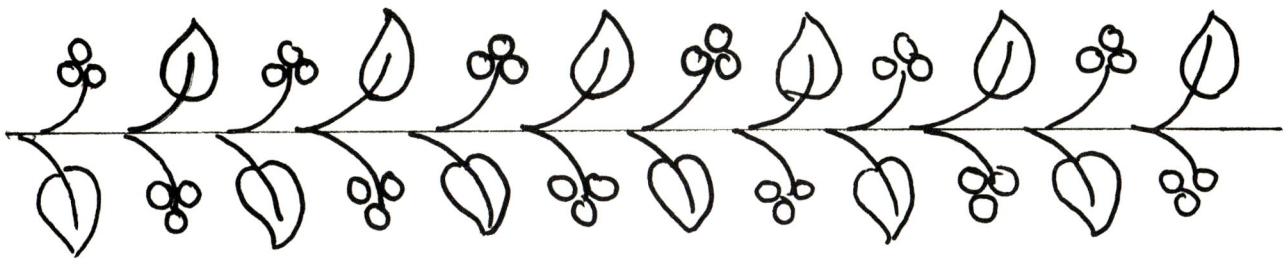

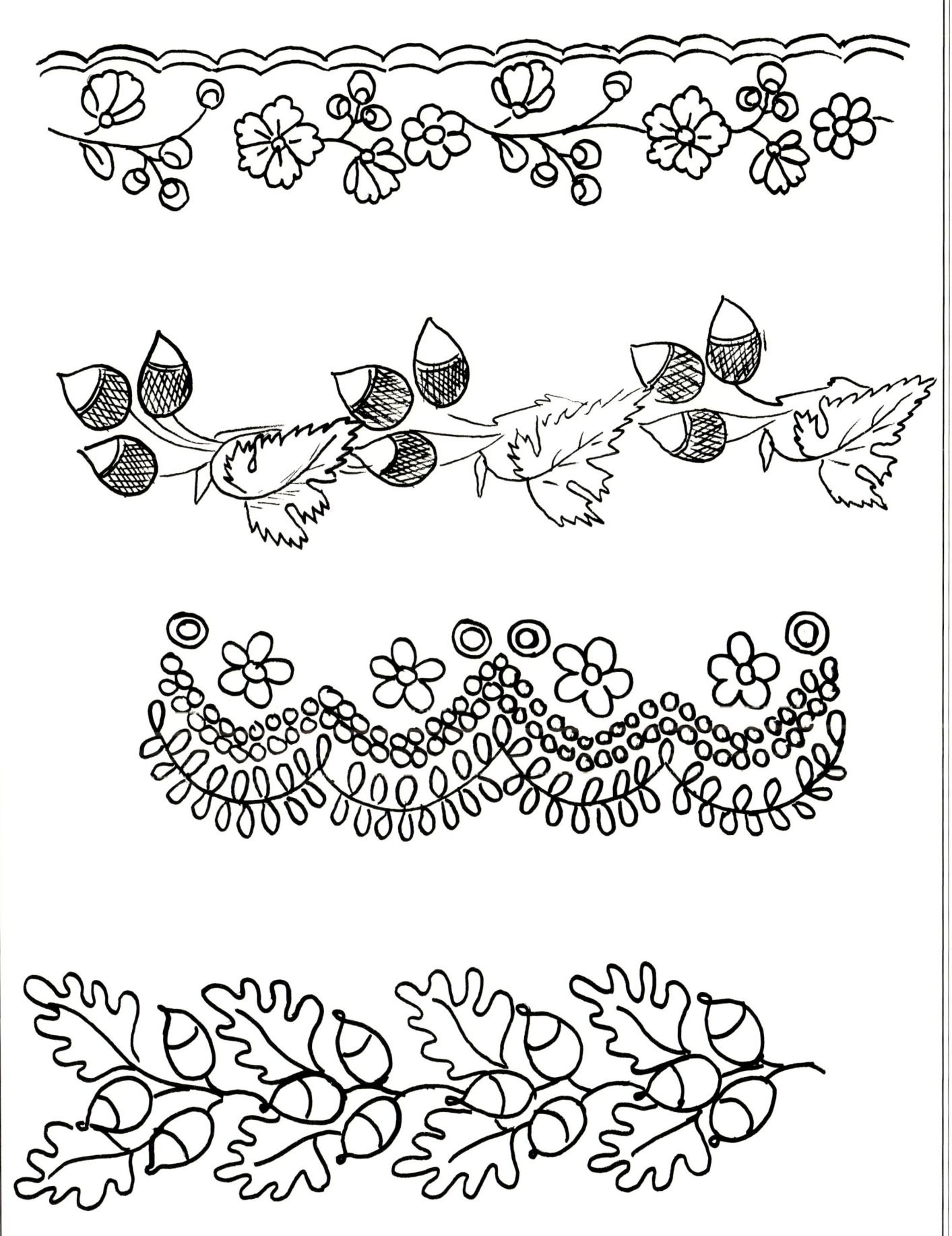

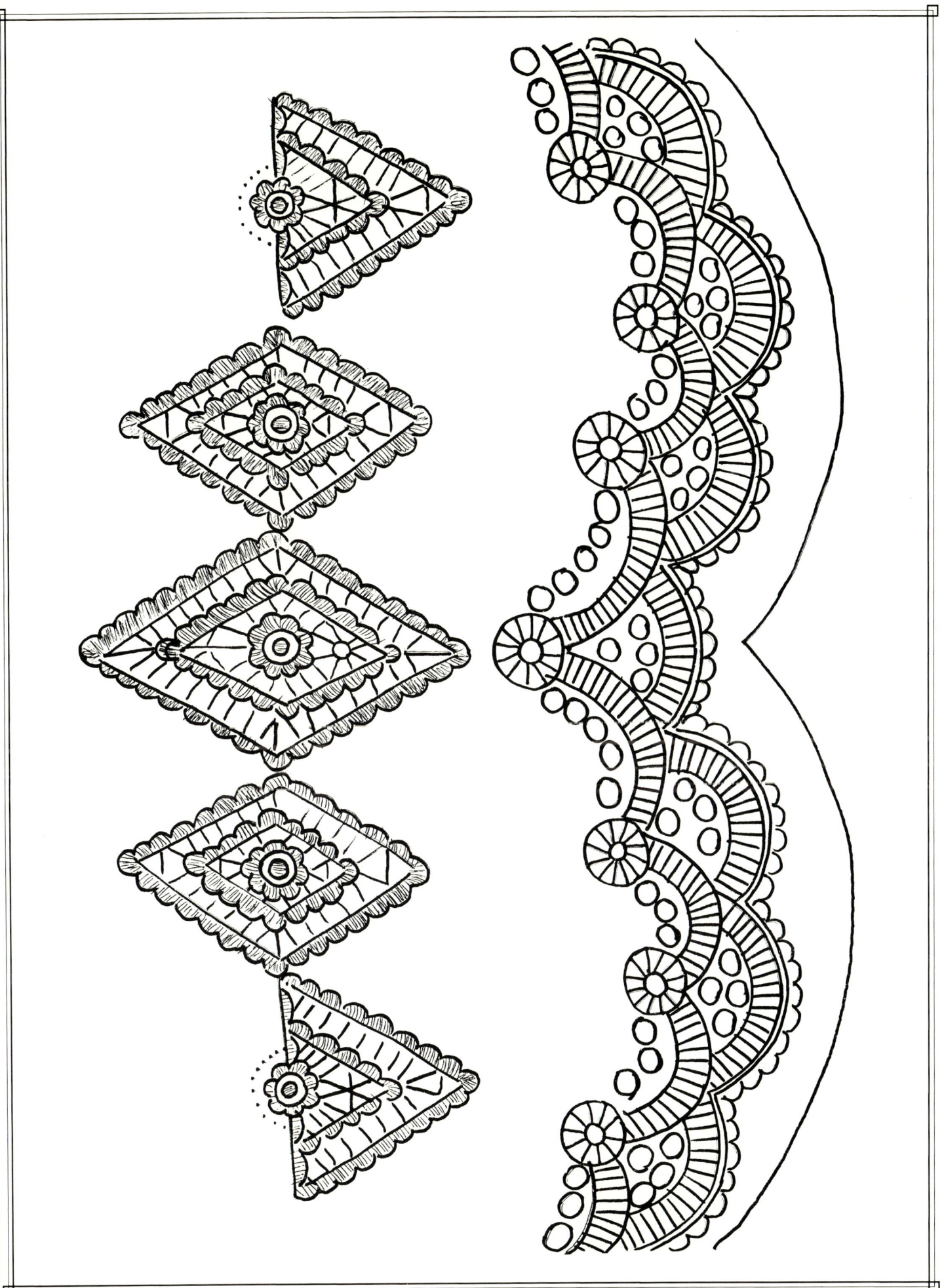

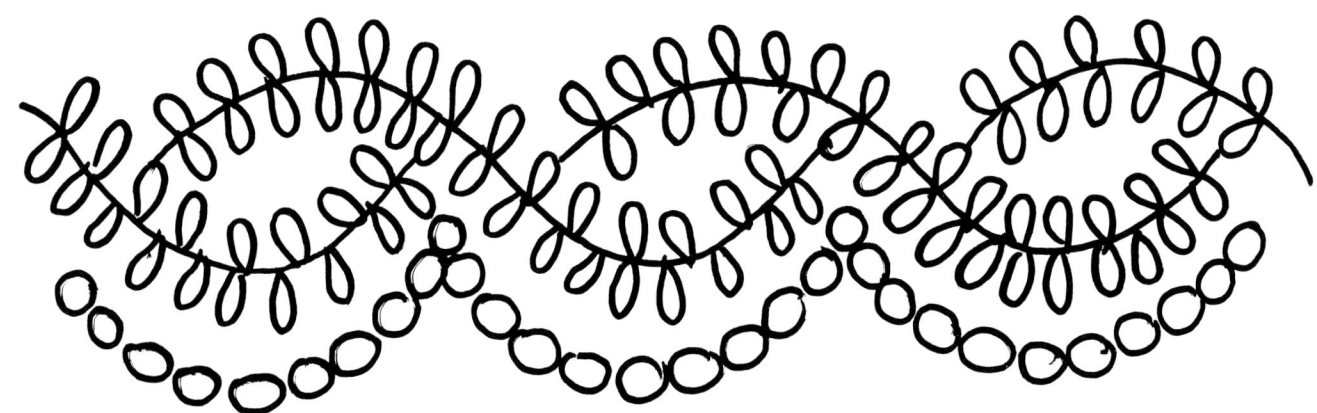

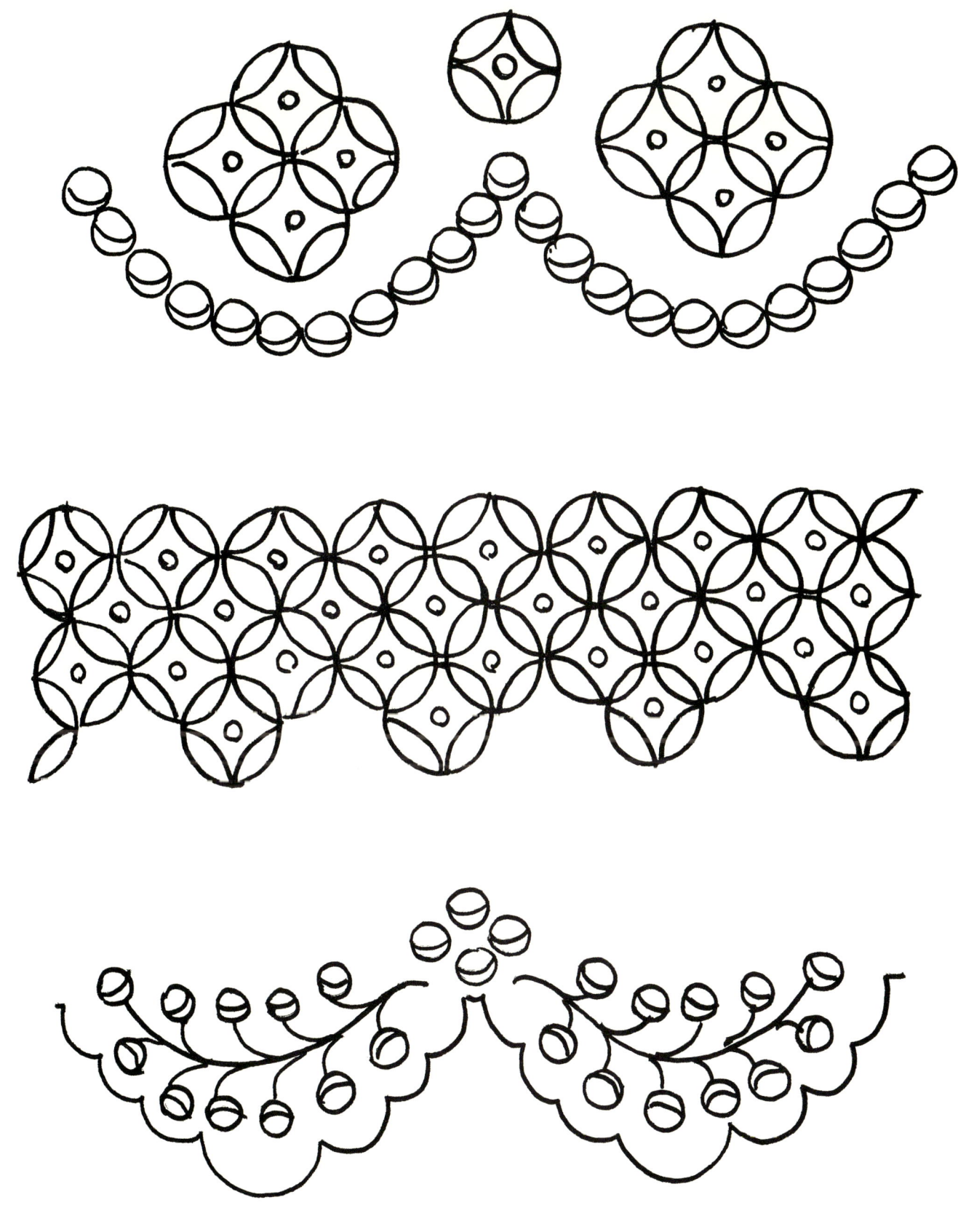

Designs for Clothing

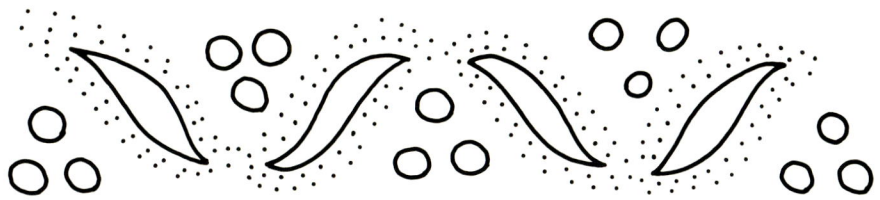

Vest Pattern

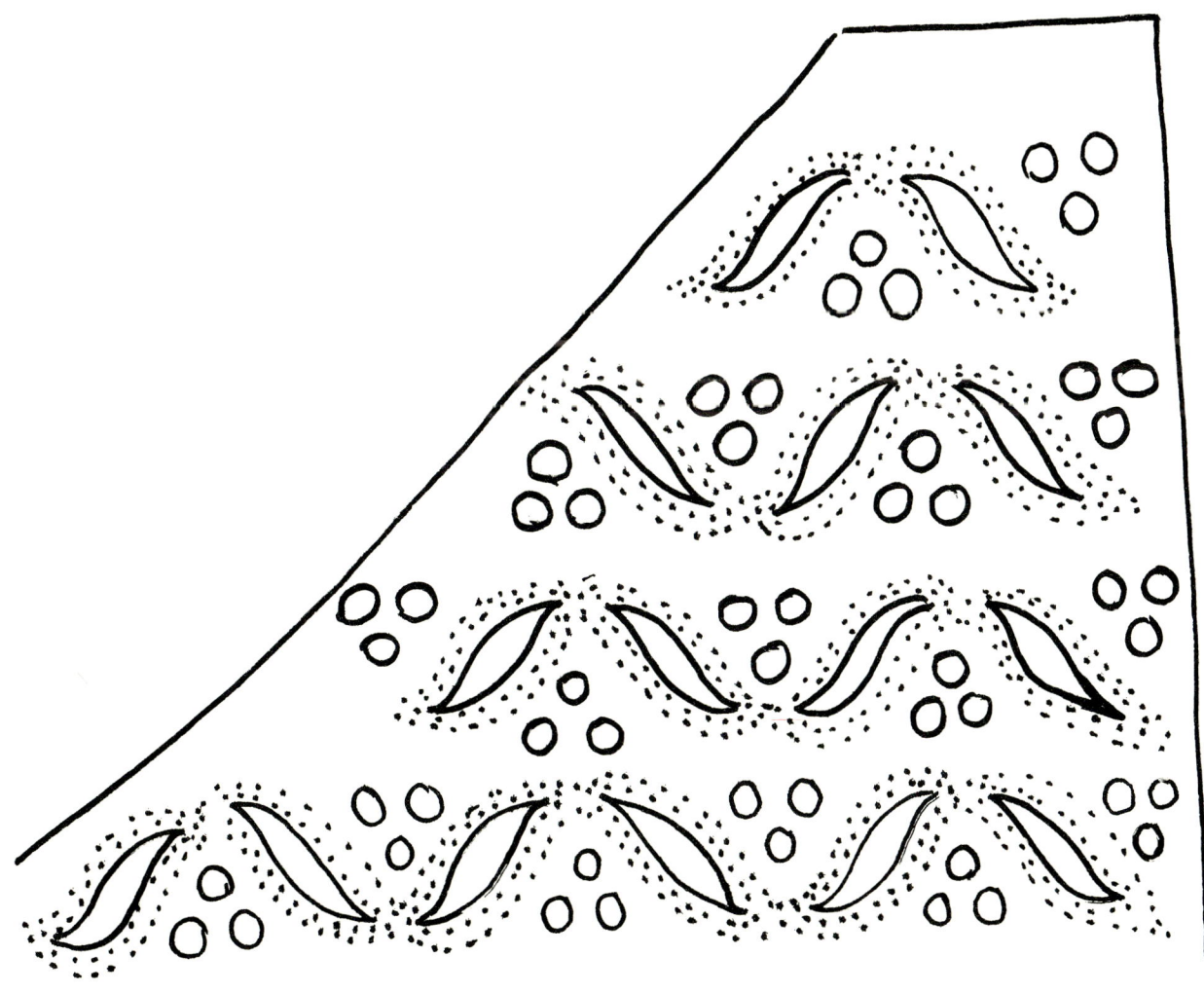

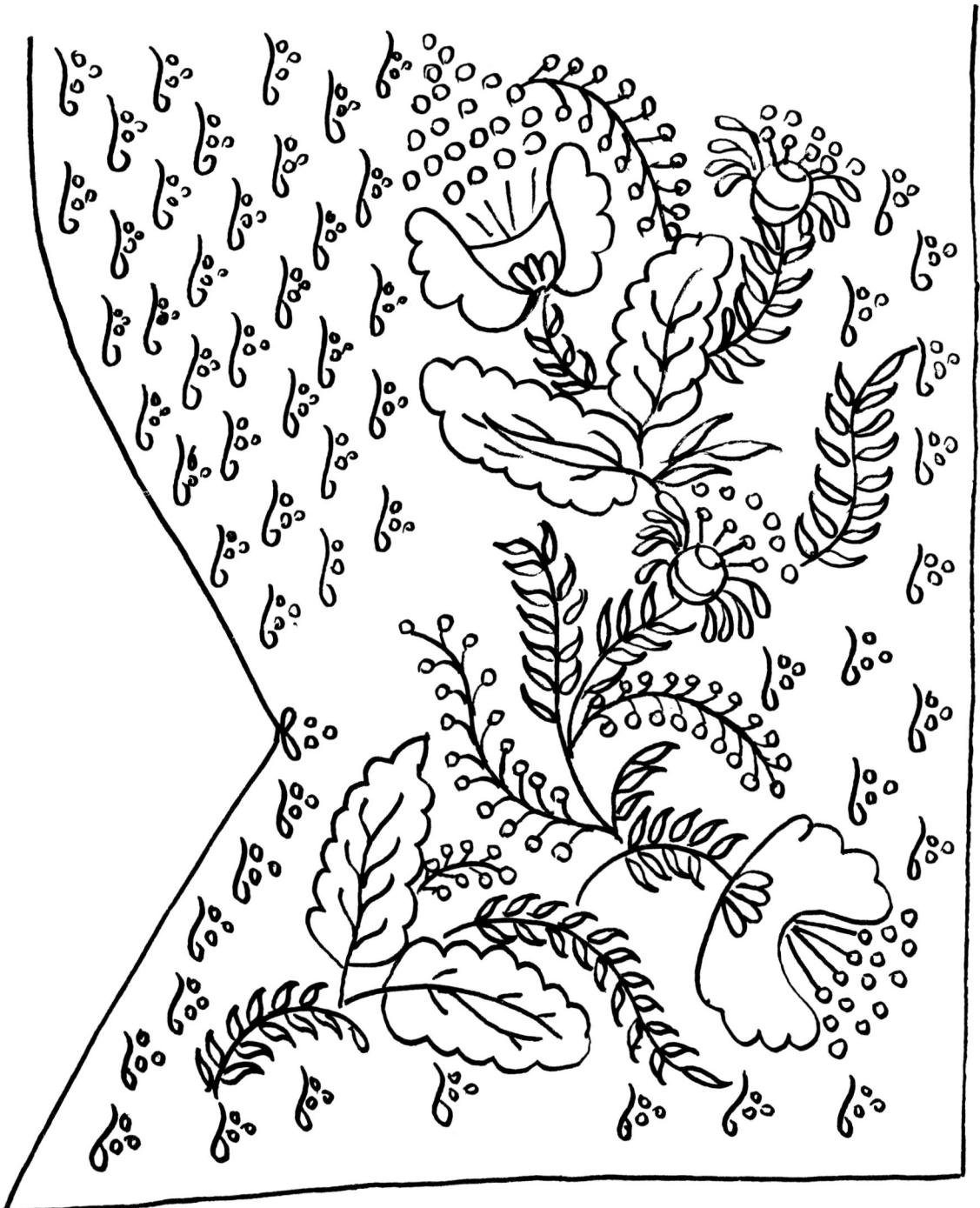

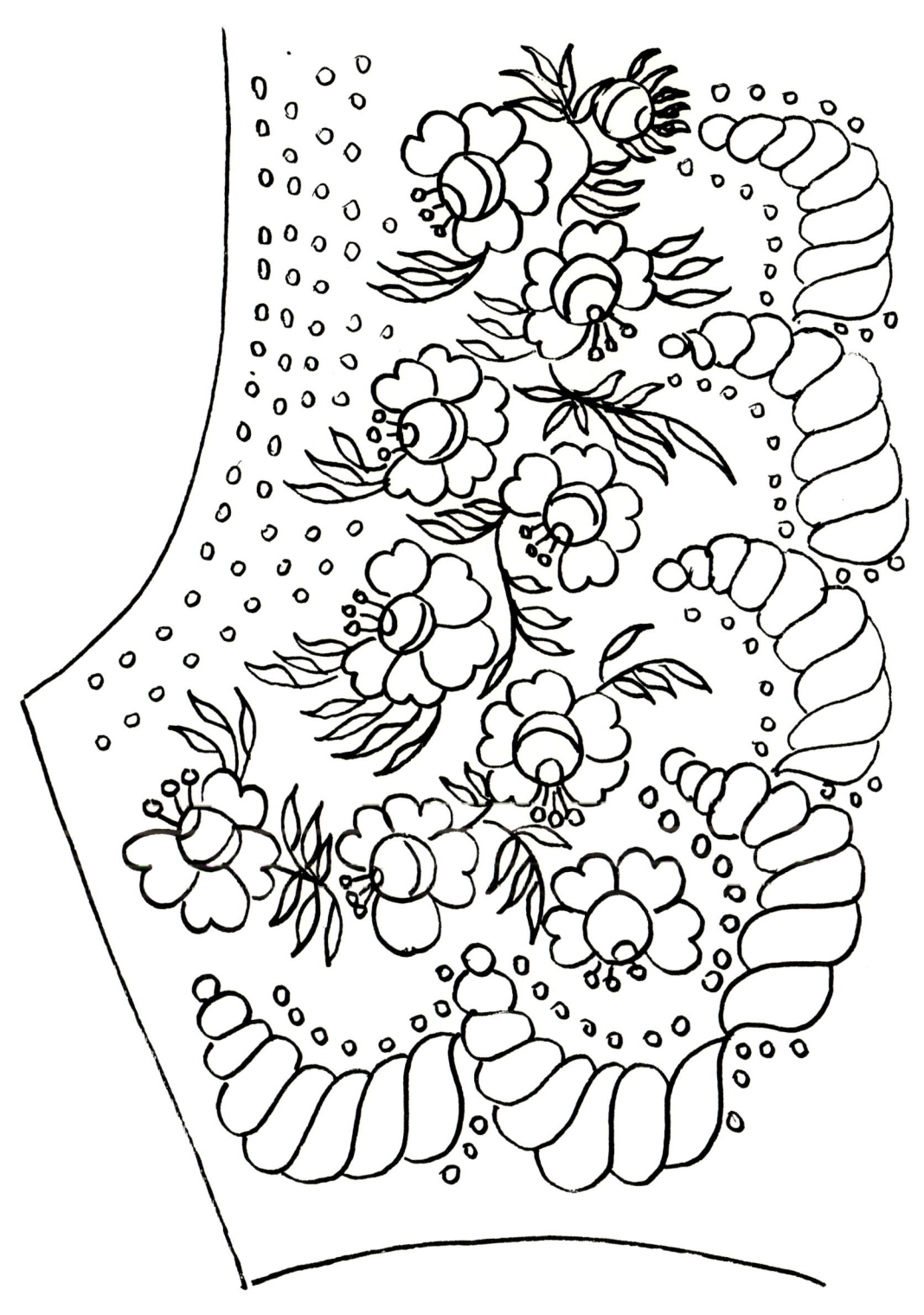

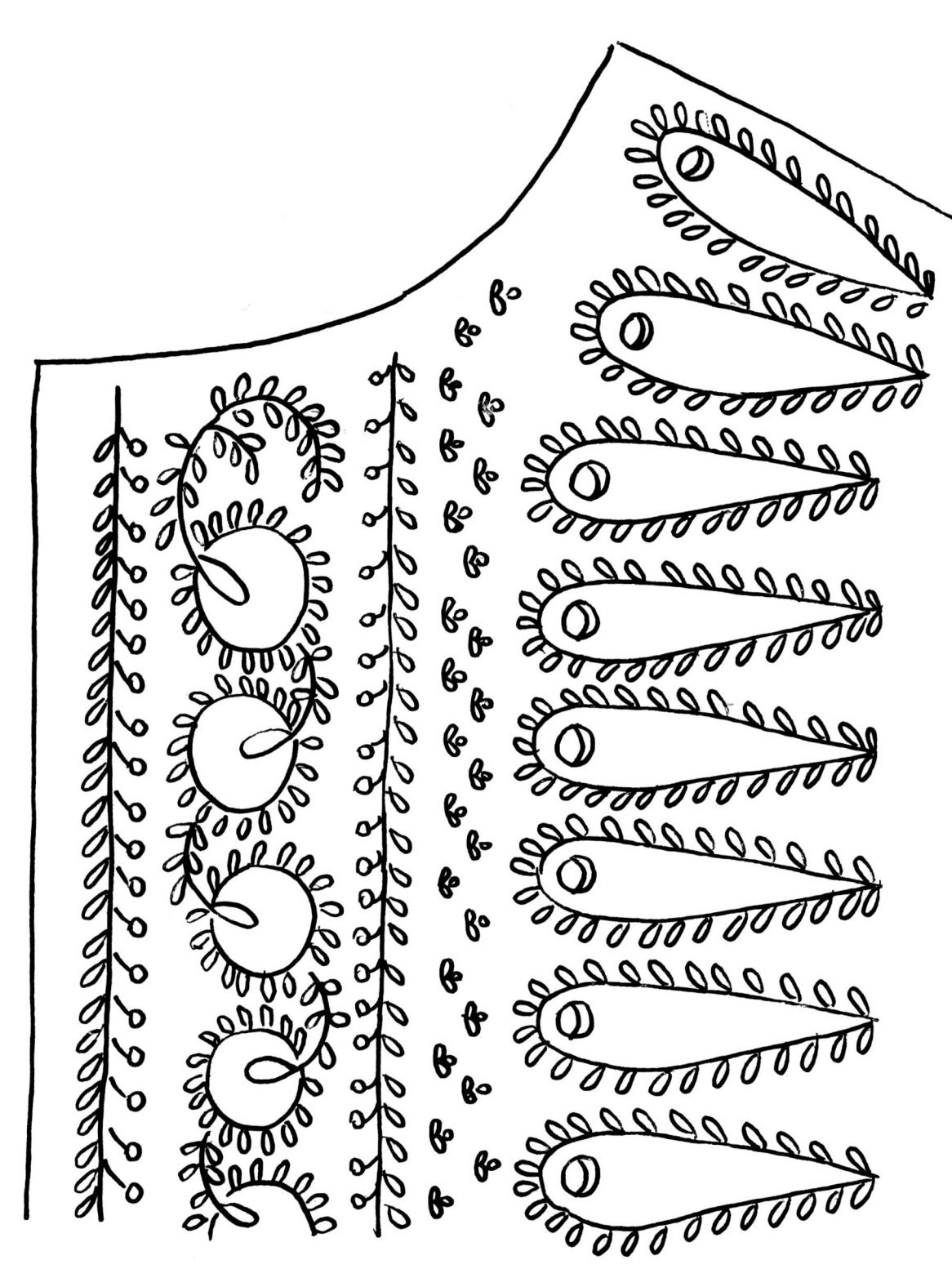

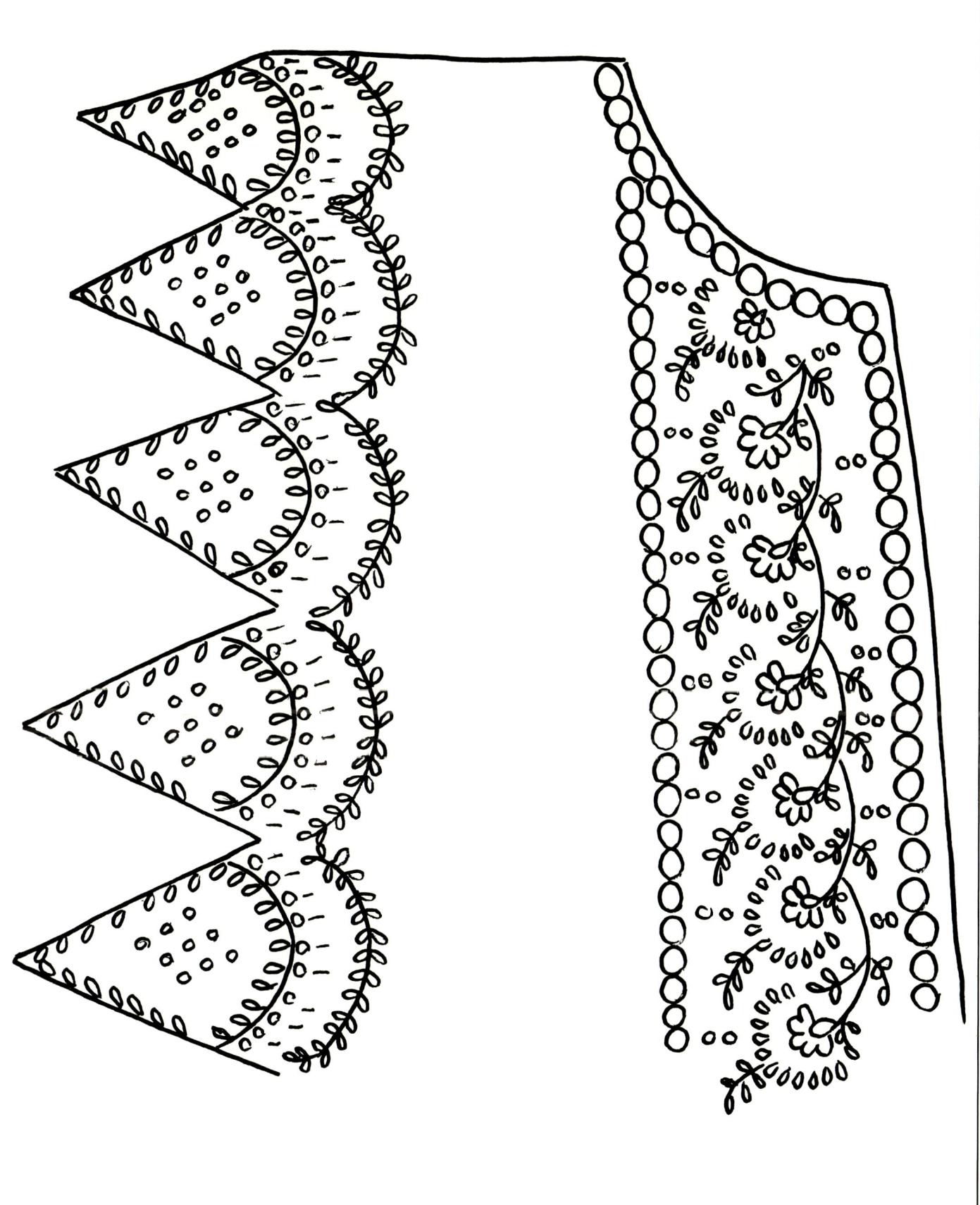

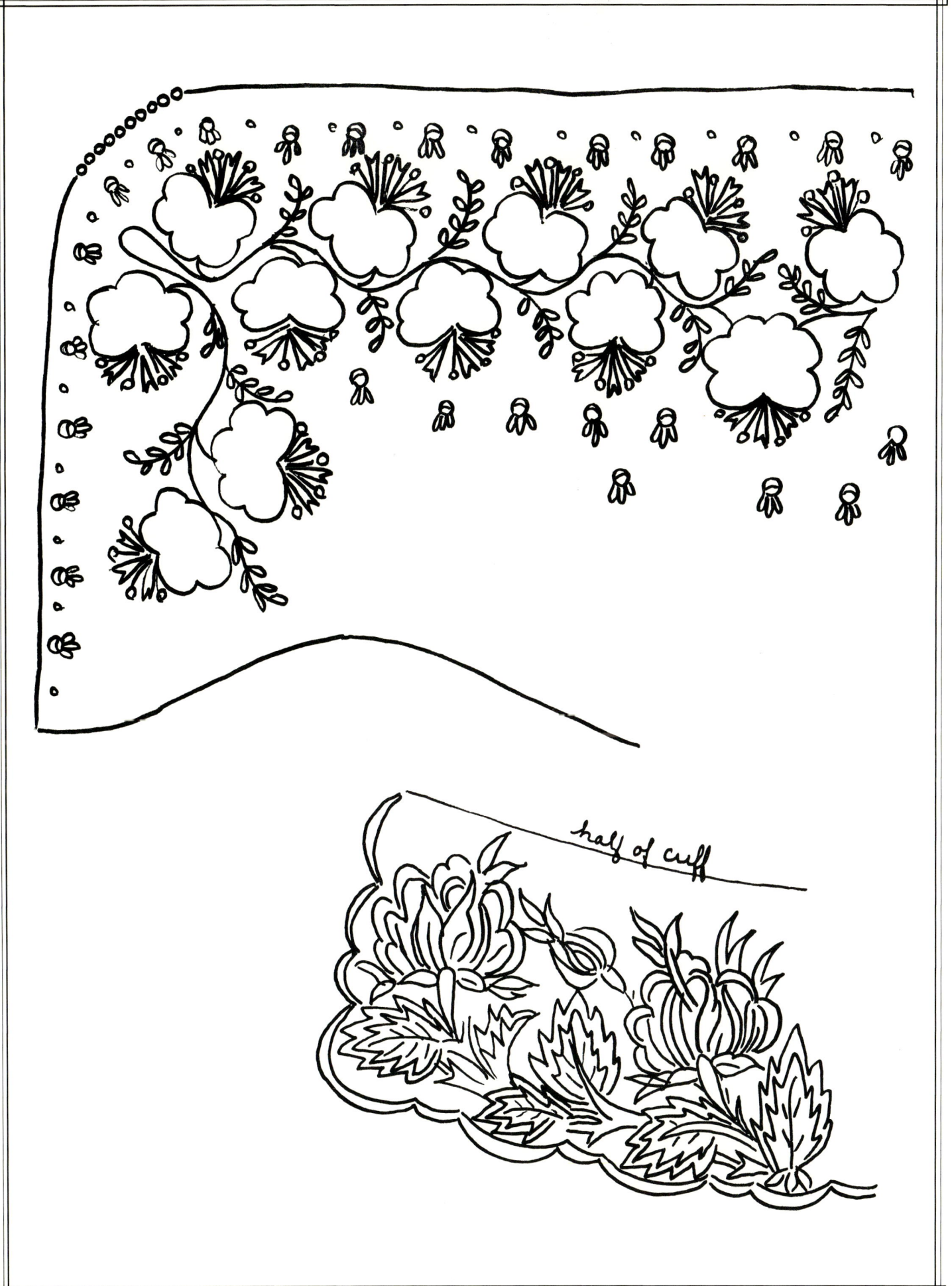

half of cuff

Half of Cuff

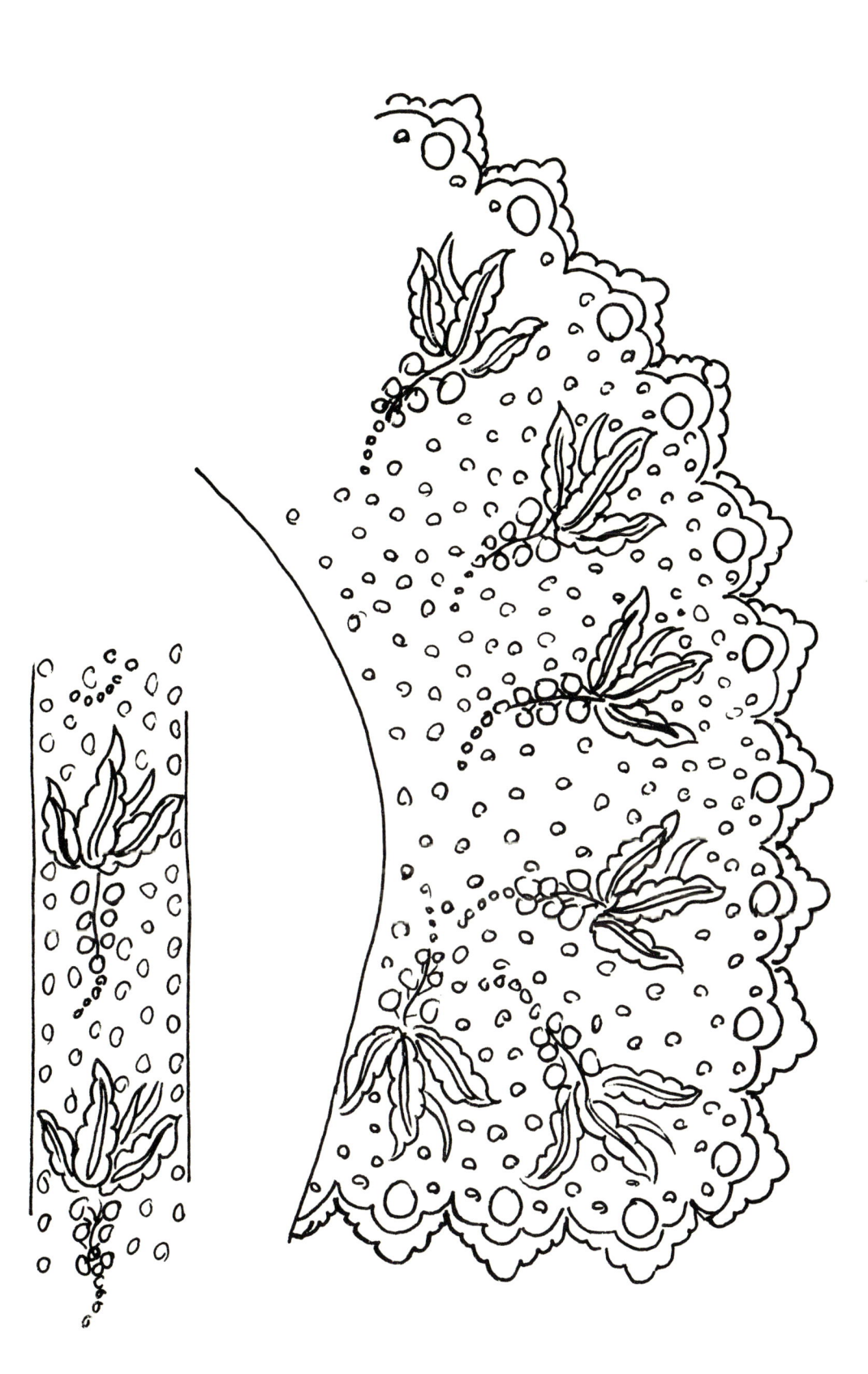

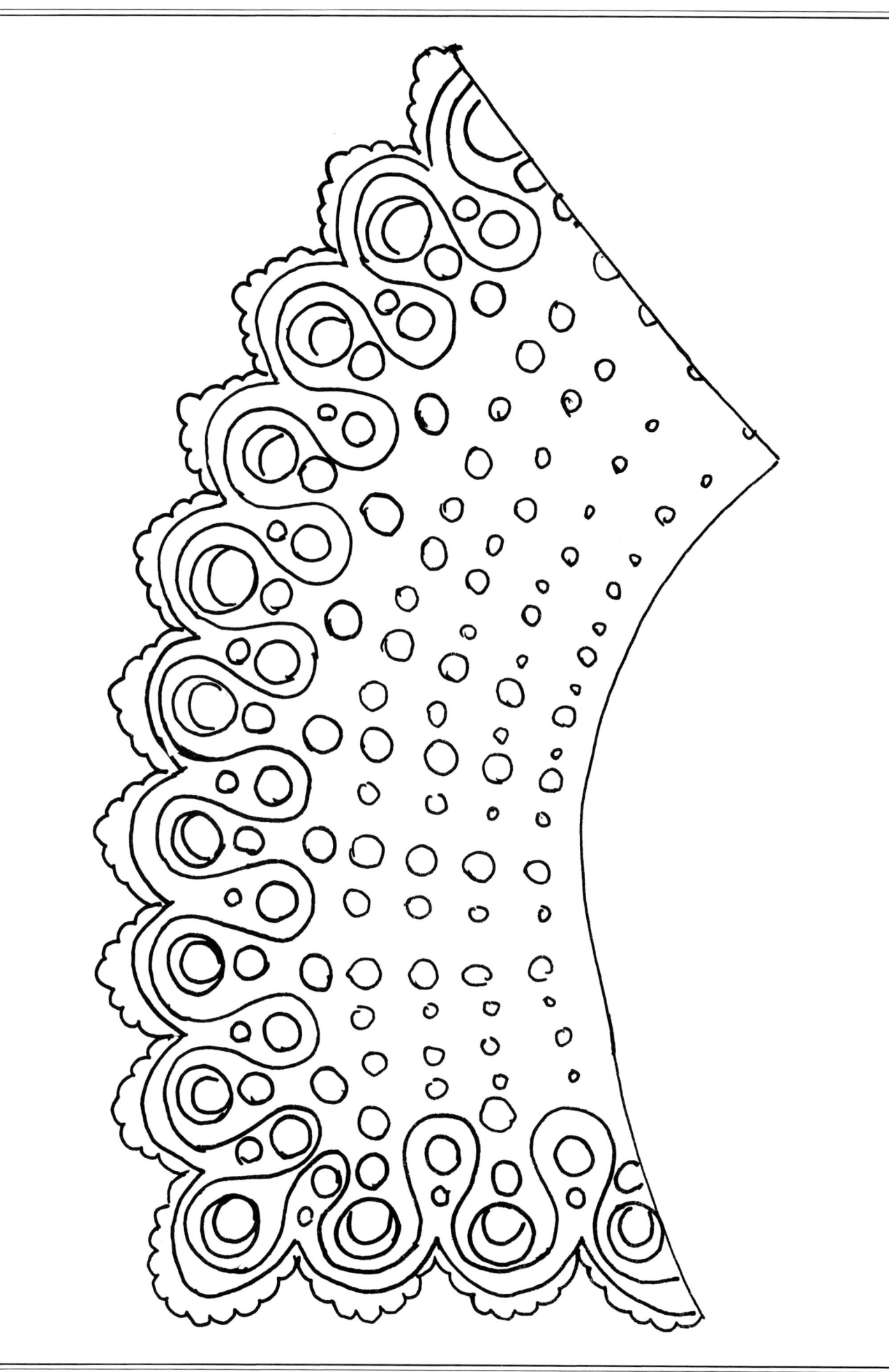

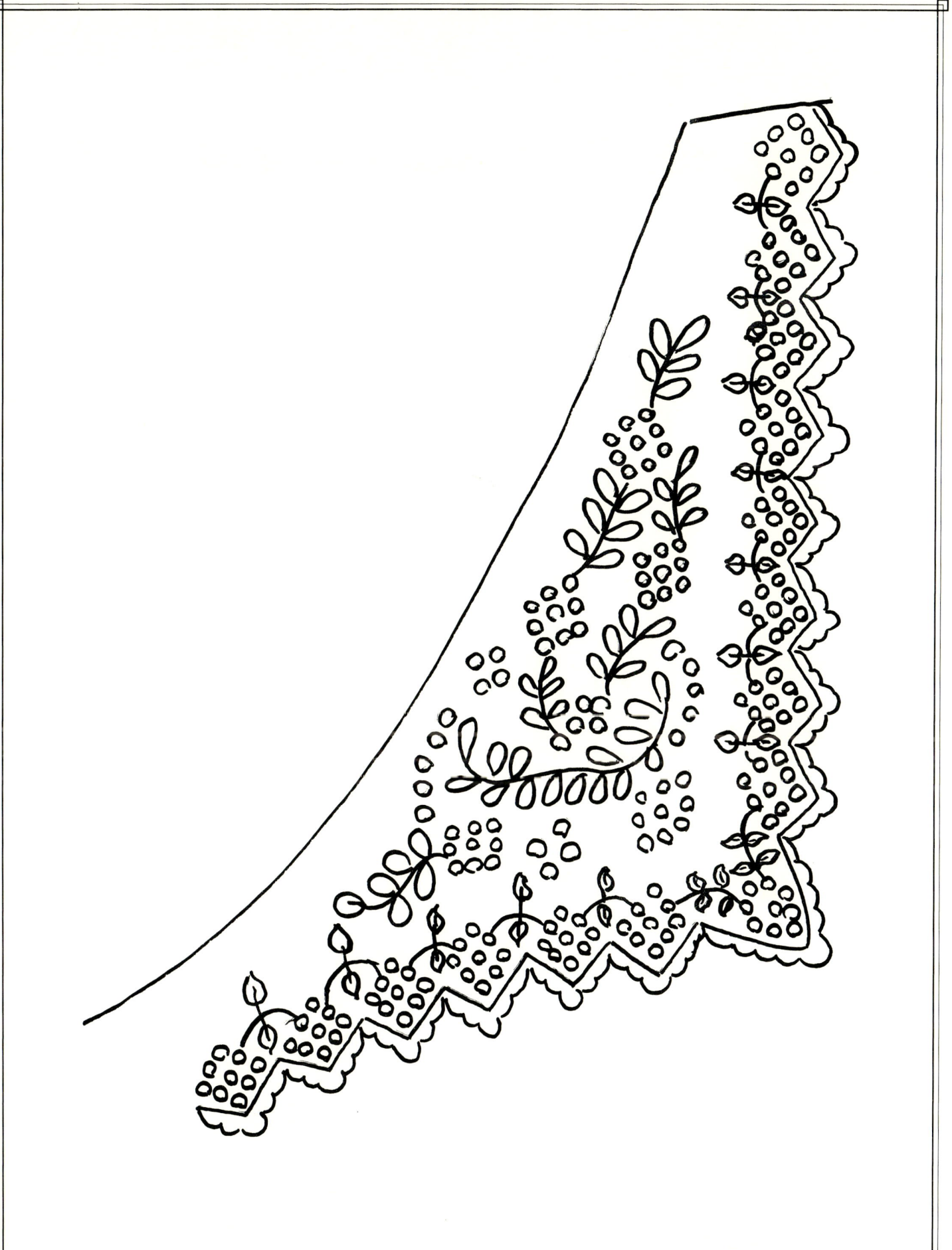

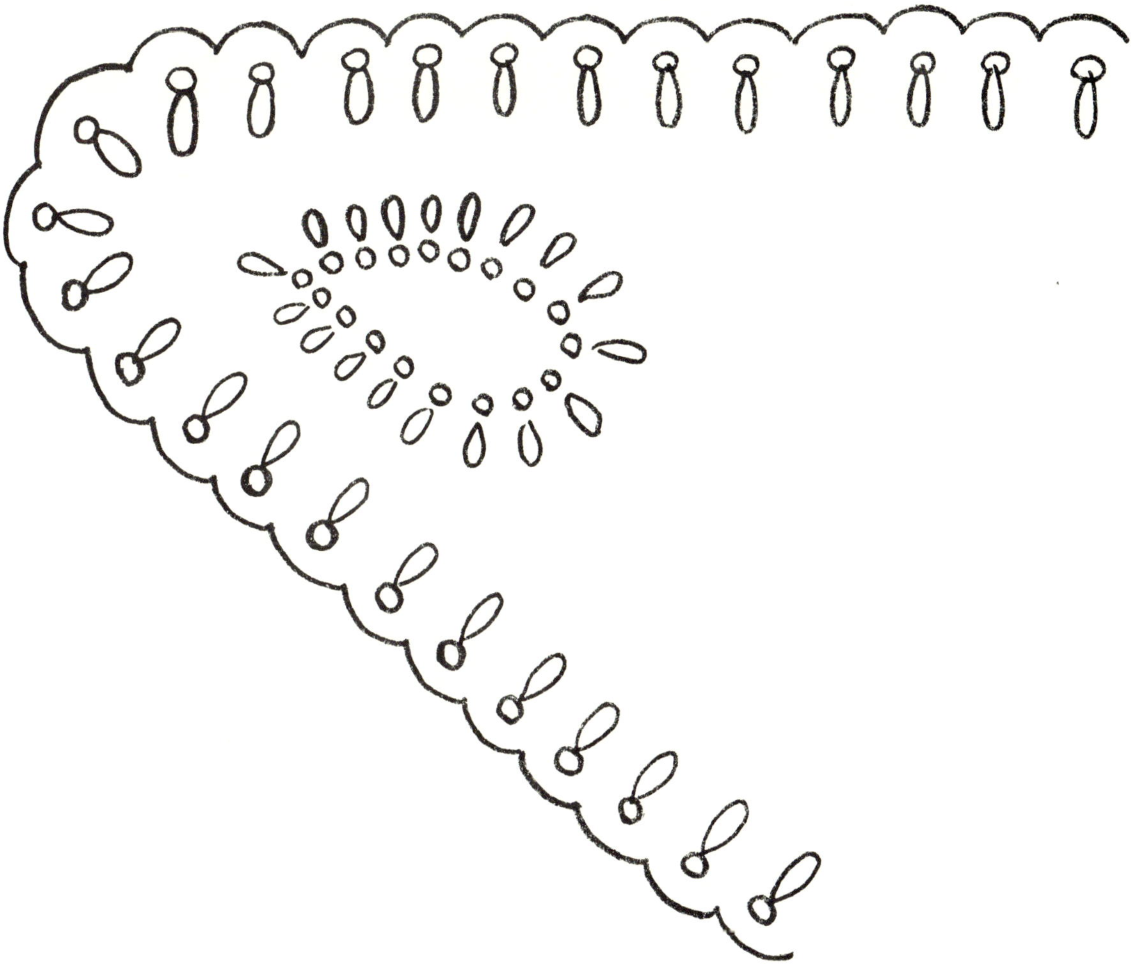

Medallions

Coronation Cord Embroidery

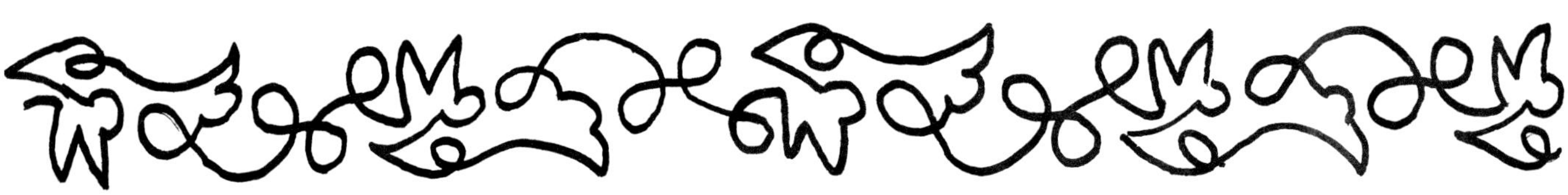

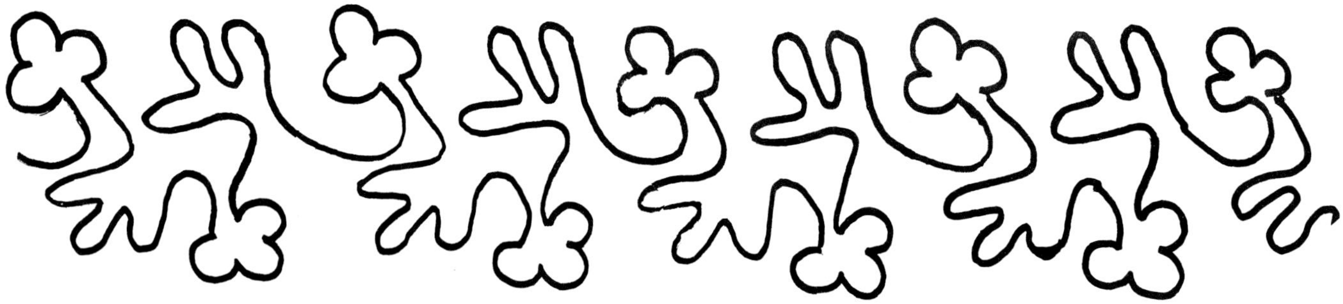

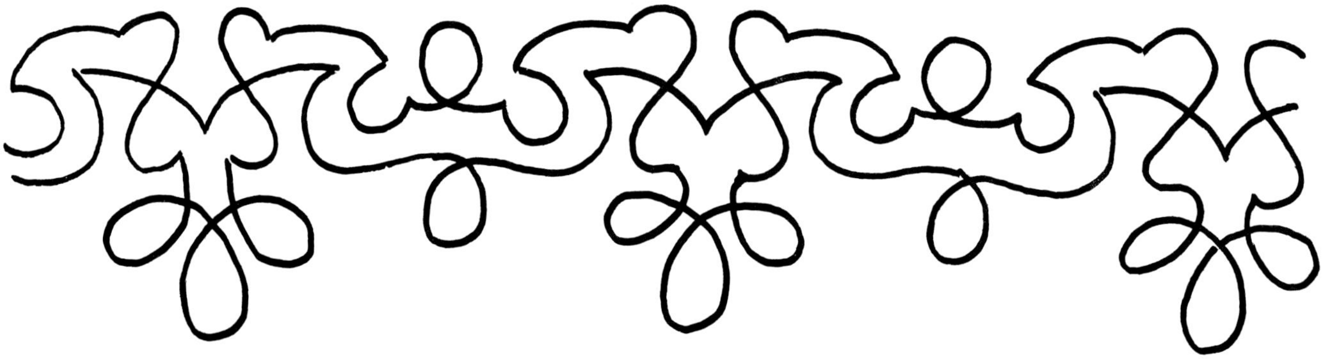

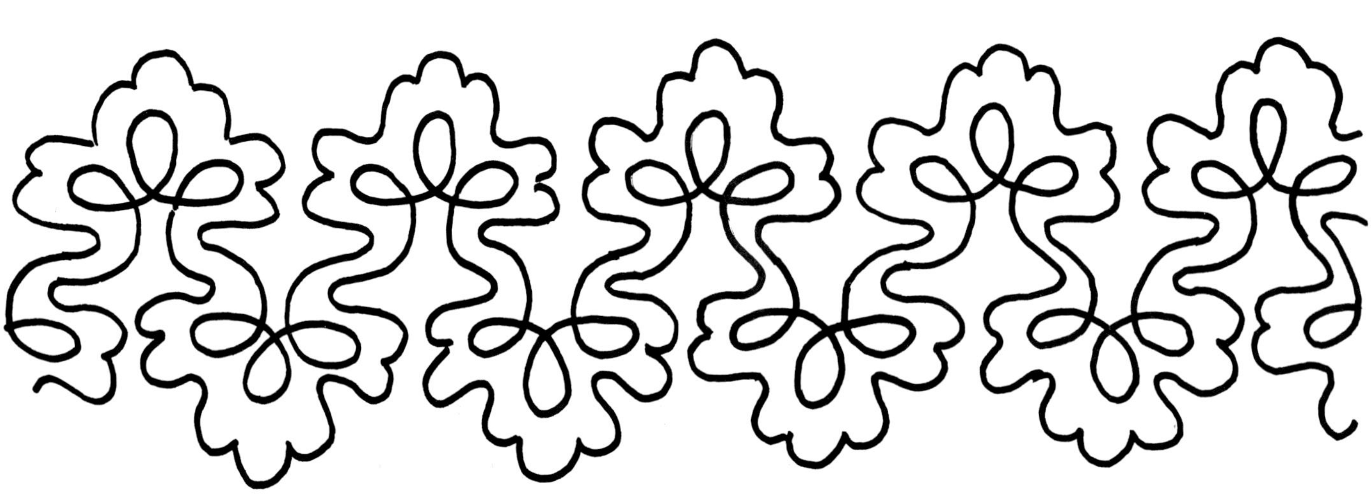

Grapes

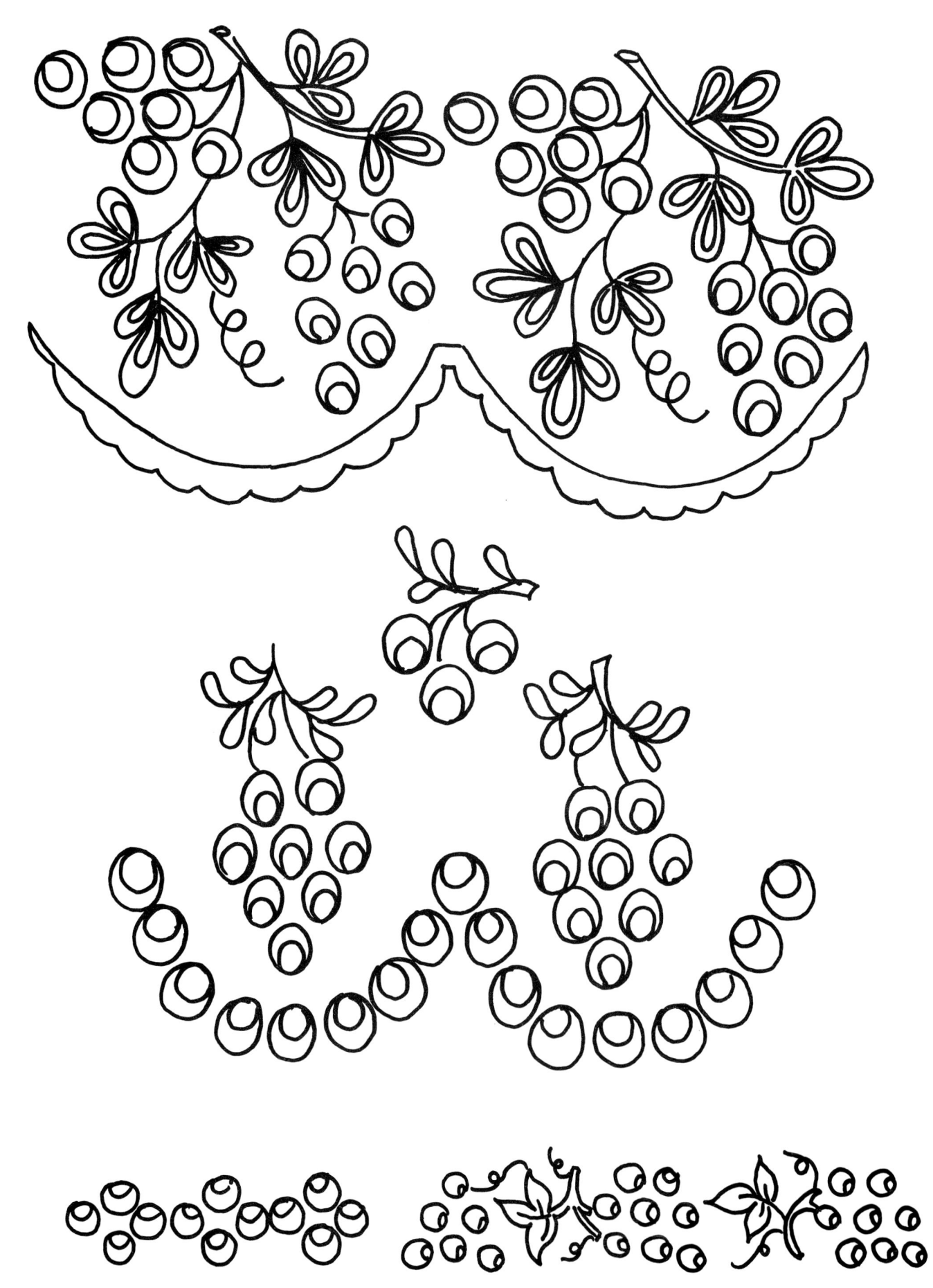

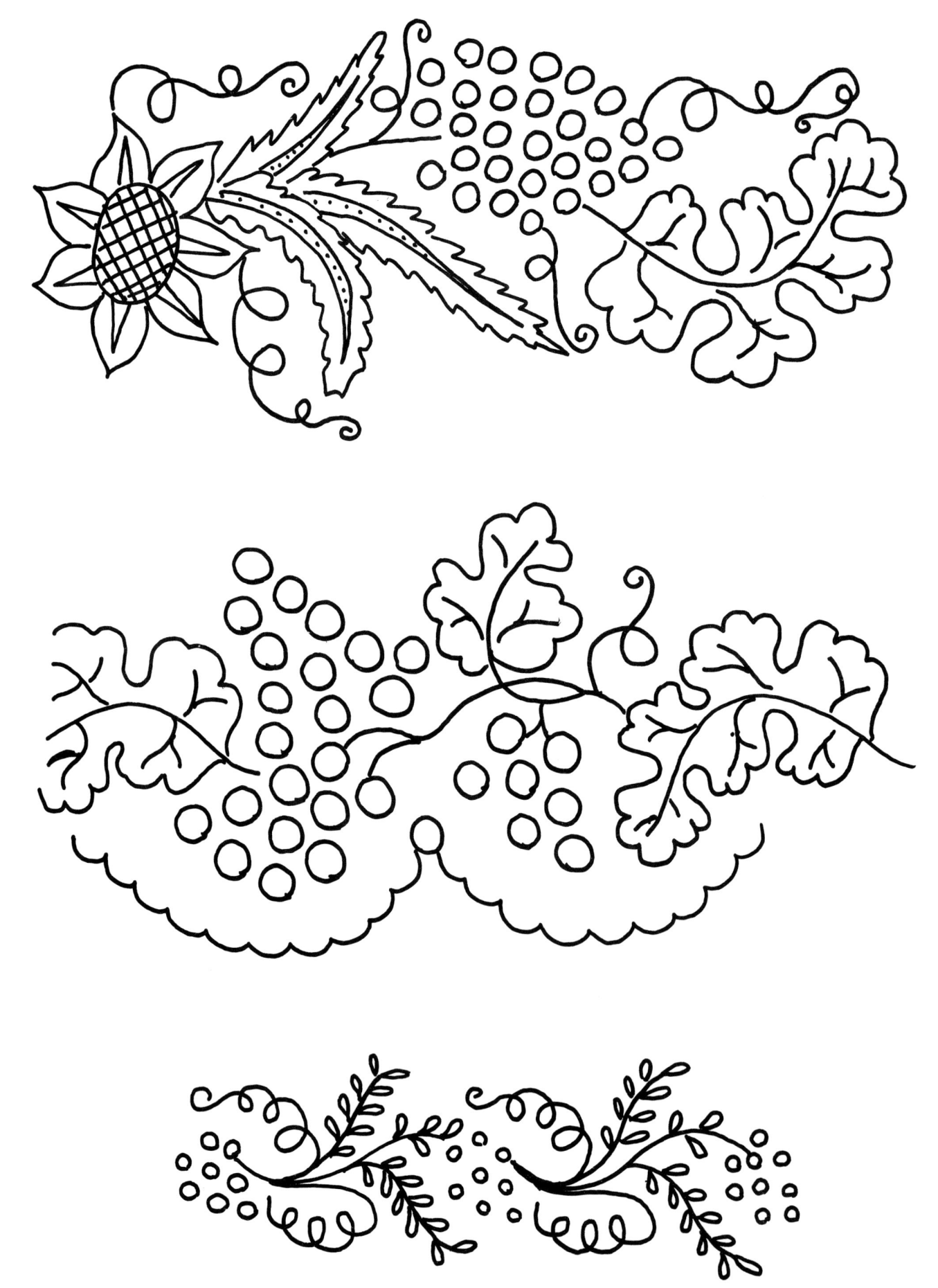

Leaves, Acorns, and Coral

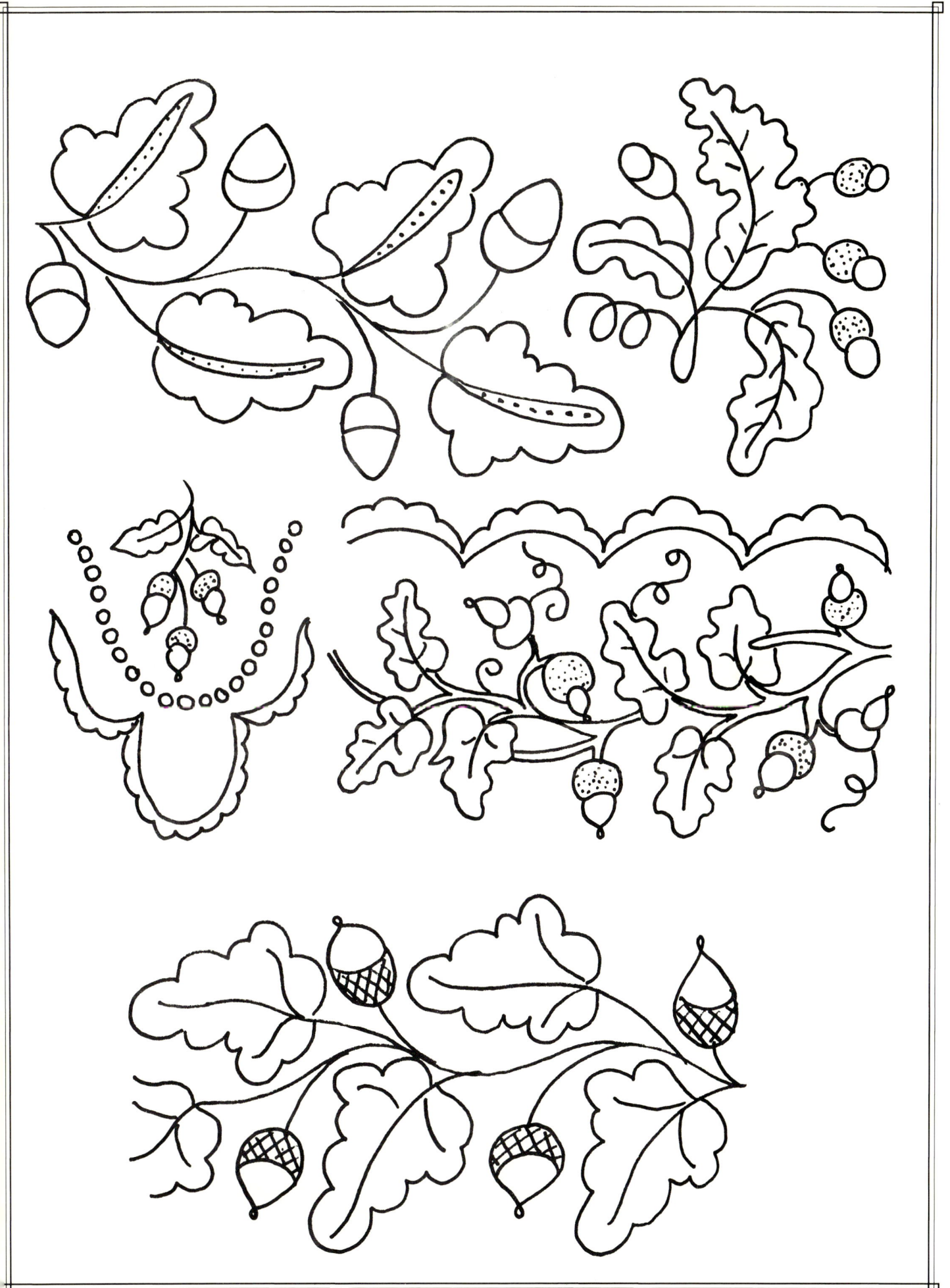

Birds and Butterflies

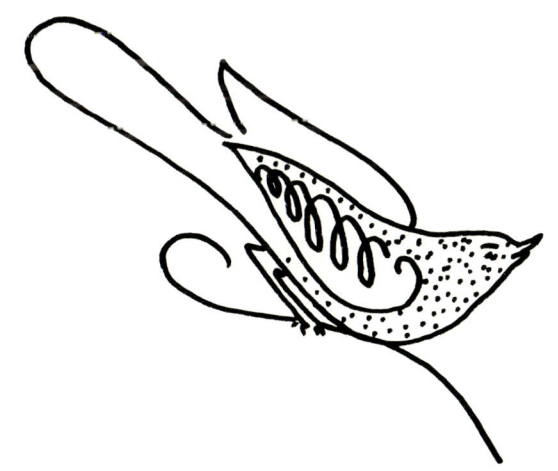

Designs for Lace

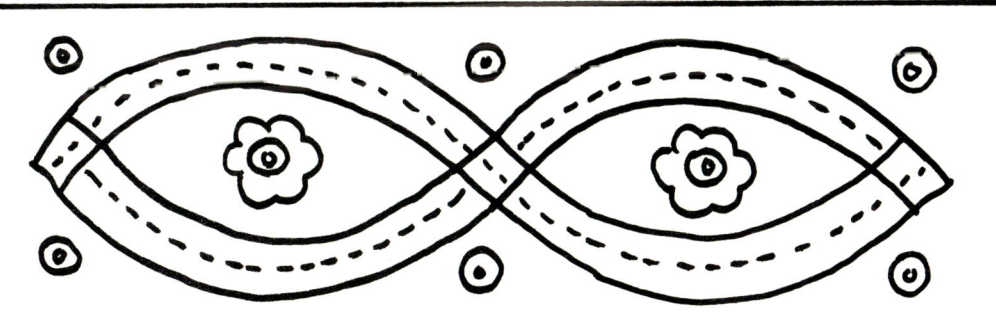

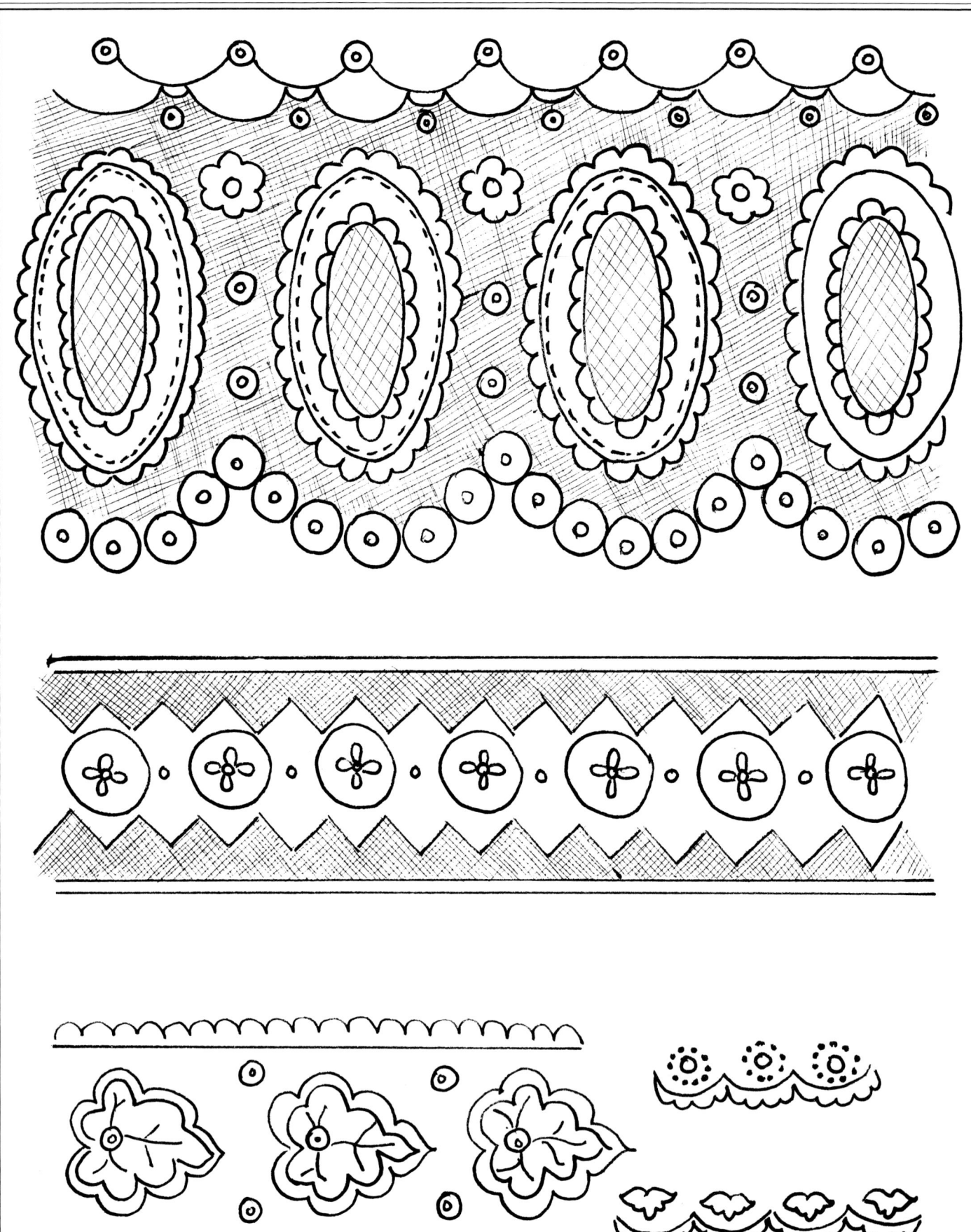

All-over Patterns

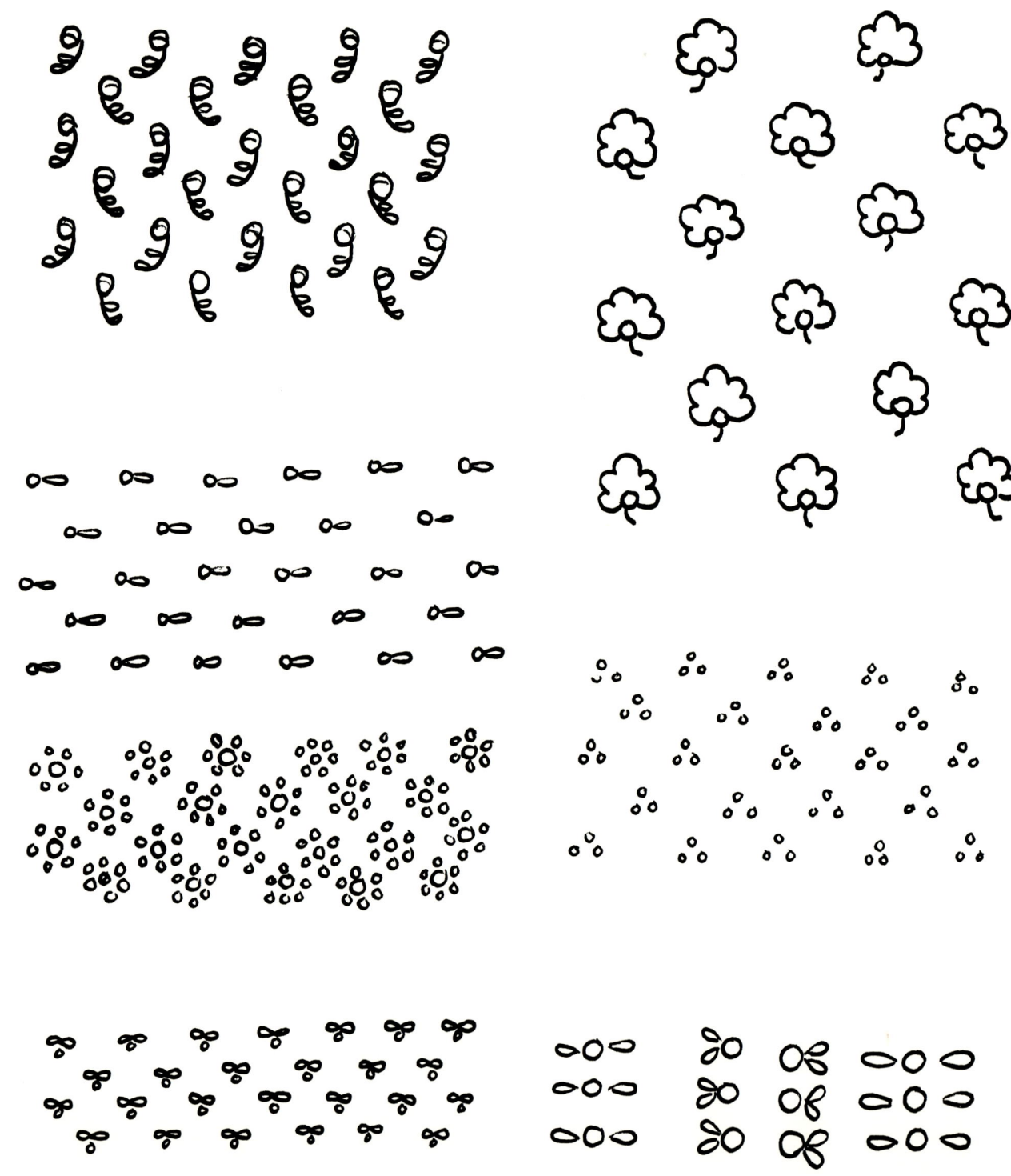

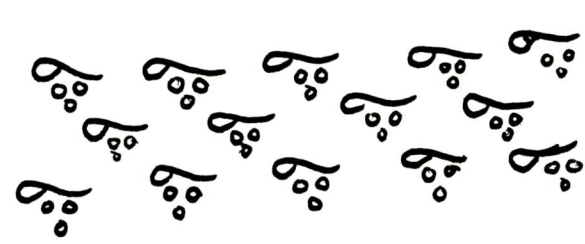

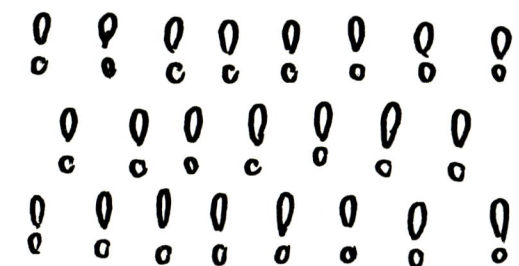

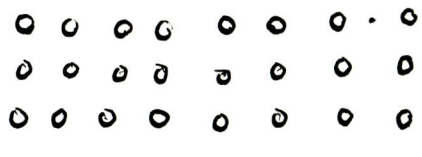

Alphabets and Letters

218

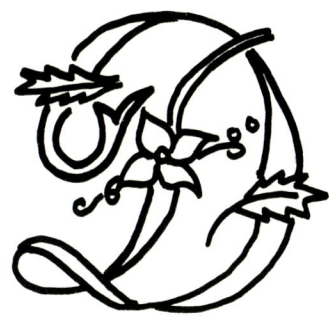

223

Appendix

Sarah J. Backerville Wamley 1858.

Whitework Embroidery Instructions

Originally the majority of these designs would have been used for whitework. The embroideries which fall under the name whitework can be enormously diverse. Perhaps the most familiar forms are broderie anglaise, Ayrshire embroidery, French and eyelet work, shadow work, drawn thread, pulled thread, and Mountmellick work. With a bit of coaxing the embroiderer might expand the list to include Hedebo, Hardanger, and the needle laces. Less familiar forms are punch work, Parma embroidery, Sardinian embroidery, Casalguidi, Armager, Blikinge, and Delsbo. Since some of these types of embroidery are little-known or little-used today, directions for many of them follow. Since the instructions for others can be found in any good stitch book, they are not repeated here.

As the name implies, all forms of whitework were originally worked on white fabric with white thread, although the category might possibly have been broadened to include natural, unbleached materials. Certainly monochrome was essential to the definition. Today, those of an experimental bent can take these old patterns, enlarge or reduce them, work them in a variety of threads unknown when the early examples were stitched, and choose a broad range of color. The purist may cringe at this thought, but embroidery thrives on adaptation, experimentation, and evolution.

Materials

The most common materials for whitework embroidery were traditionally linens and cottons. Silks were sometimes used for all-white work. Later came rayon thread, which was sometimes labeled in French, *soie artificielle*, possibly in the hope that the buyer might understand the translation of silk, yet miss the designation as artificial.

We still have available a variety of weights and types of linen and cotton fabrics and threads. A list of suppliers is included to help in finding suitable materials. Neither the quality nor the variety of a hundred years ago exists today, but there is still an ample selection which should satisfy most stitchers. Cotton threads available today which are typical of the ones formerly used: stranded cotton (also known as floss); coton à broder, sizes 12, 16, 25; matte cotton, size 4; floche à broder, size 25; cotton sewing and lace threads in fine sizes; pearl cotton, sizes 3, 5, 8, 12.

Most of these are supplied by the DMC Corporation, and are imported from France. Other manufacturers make one or more of the products. The supply of linen is not so broad, being restricted to linen lace thread, a few brands of wet-spun threads imported from Scandinavia, and some wet-spun and dry-spun threads distributed by one American manufacturer.

Use a doodle cloth and experiment to see which threads will best suit your purposes. Keep in mind that a final experiment before embarking on your project should be worked with the actual thread on the actual fabric proposed.

Remember always that no amount of skill will ever overcome some of the problems that can be caused by the use of poor quality materials. Use the best that you can find. This becomes even more than ordinarily important if the finished piece is to be used for a garment and will be subjected to the rigors of repeated washing.

Transferring the Designs

The method of transferring the designs will vary from fabric to fabric, but in most cases you begin by making a copy of the design on good-quality tracing paper.

Prick and pounce

Place the traced design over a piece of pricking paper. Put the two together on a pad of felt or cork, and prick the outlines with a very fine needle. Special tools, called prickers, are available for holding the needle. They are generally used by lacemakers. An alternative is a pin vice.

pin vice

Next lay the fabric on the felt or cork board and position the pricked design over it, securing both carefully so that they will not slip. Rub powdered charcoal or chalk over the pricked paper, working it into the holes. Lift the paper, and gently shake the excess powder from the fabric. With an indelible, or removable, marker of your choice, go over the outline.

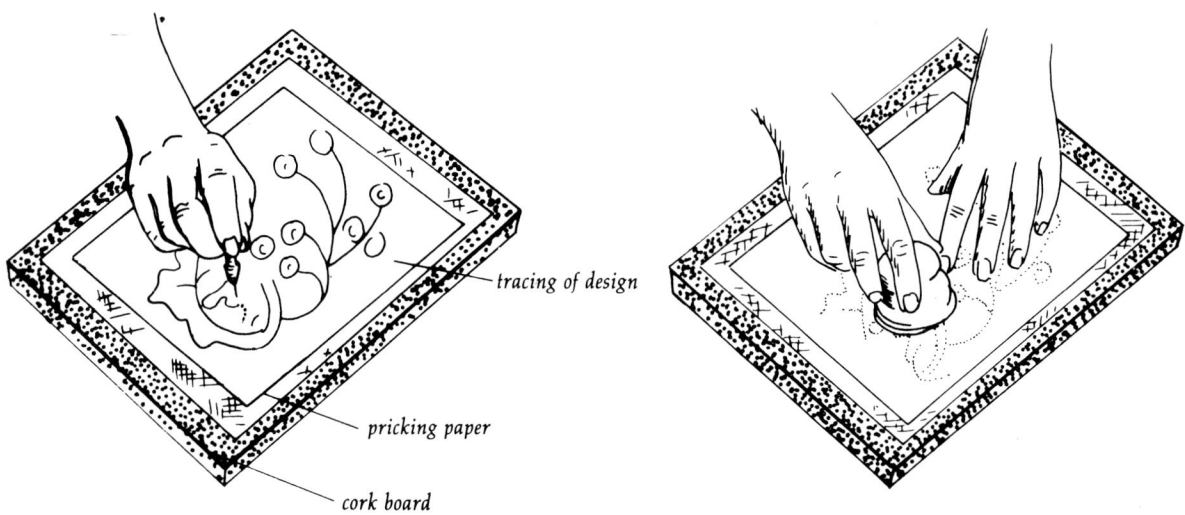

tracing of design

pricking paper

cork board

Tracing

If your fabric is thin, you can lay it over a design and trace directly onto the fabric with a sharp, hard lead pencil, water-erasable marker, or India ink pen.

Carbon paper

Center the tracing of the diagram over the fabric and pin it to the fabric with a few pins placed along the top side of the design only. Slip a piece of graphite carbon paper between the fabric and the pattern. Secure all to a smooth, firm surface. Trace over the outlines with a worn-out ballpoint pen, a knitting needle, a stylus or a pencil. When you have traced a few lines, lift the paper and carbon to see if you are pressing hard enough.

Light table

This method requires a light table or a glass-top table. Pin your tracing securely underneath the fabric, centering carefully. Place the sandwich on the light table, and trace over the lines with an India ink pen or water-erasable marker.

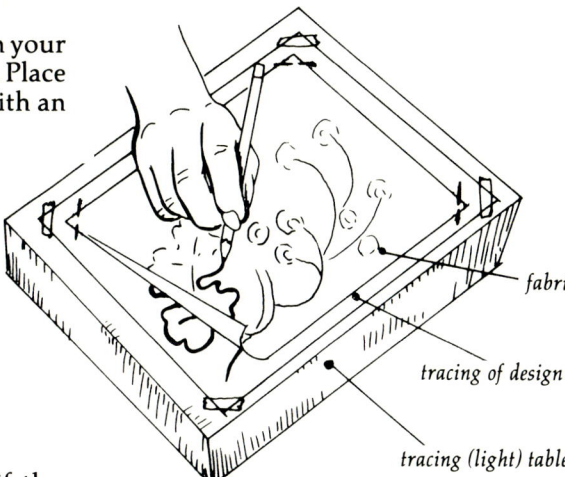

fabric

tracing of design

tracing (light) table

Basting

Pin the tracing to the fabric. This method works best if the fabric is firmly held in a frame, to avoid any shifting. Stitch over all the lines of the design with sewing thread in the color of the fabric. Use a running stitch in which most of the thread lies on the surface of the fabric and only a short stitch is made on the reverse side. After all the design lines have been stitched, tear and remove the paper. A pair of burling irons, or tweezers, is very helpful in getting out the last tiny bits. This method is a good one to use if you are not absolutely sure of your design. Outlines can be changed at any time by removing a basting thread.

Making your own iron-on transfer

There are pencils for making iron-on transfers, which can sometimes be found in needlework shops. They come in magenta and yellow. To use one, trace your design and go over all the lines of the tracing ON THE REVERSE SIDE OF THE PAPER. You will have made a hot-iron transfer, which can be used like any purchased one would be. Make a test sample and try it first. These pencils do not work on every fabric, and it is very hard to keep a good, sharp point on them. The outlines wash out of some fabric and not out of others.

Equipment

Good quality materials go hand in hand with good quality equipment. Any basic list of equipment for surface stitchery includes one each of 4, 5, and 6 embroidery hoops with screw adjustment, preferably wooden. For delicate fabrics, some embroiderers feel that it is best to wrap the inside ring with washed muslin. This protects the fabric from abrasion by the hoop, as well as prevents the fabric from slipping. Most whitework techniques depend on keeping the fabric quite taut in the hoop. A larger wooden hoop with a floor, table, or sit-on stand is very nice for working big pieces. Some stitchers prefer to use a slate frame or to thumbtack their fabric to stretcher frames. (It is best not to staple the fabric, as it will stretch in working and requires occasional tightening.)

Fine-pointed scissors, an assortment of needles, a strawberry emery, and a thimble (if you like to use one) complete the list of necessary items. Remember to wash your hands before you begin to stitch. Smokers are cautioned to wash their hands before returning to their work after having a cigarette, as the nicotine stains from their hands are particularly hard to remove.

Stitches

The directions which follow do not begin to include all the stitches which can be used to interpret the patterns in this book. Virtually any stitch can be used, particularly in translating the designs into embroidery forms other than that for which they were originally conceived. Instructions are not given for stitches which may be found in numerous other books. Among those which are not included are back stitch, bullion knots, chain stitch, cretan, French knots, long and short stitch, rope stitch, running stitch, satin stitch, spider webs, split stitch, stem or outline, whipped back stitch, and whipped stem or outline. The ones which are included were selected because they were less familiar or appeared in fewer books.

Buttonhole Edges

This stitch is often used to finish table or bed linens or at the neck, armholes, or hem of undergarments. If it is to be used to finish a garment in this way, assemble the garment before doing the buttonhole edges, so that the stitching can be worked continuously. Carefully calculate the small additional amount of fabric which must be allowed at each edge to be finished in this way, and cut outside the basic pattern shape to provide this amount.

Transfer the design to the fabric. To raise, or pad, the buttonhole stitch, begin by working several rows of running stitch as illustrated by the diagram.

To begin your buttonhole stitch, anchor the thread by taking a few running stitches in the padded area.

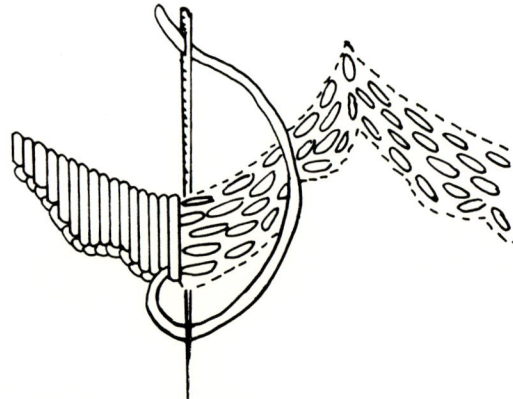

Care should be taken to keep each stitch perpendicular to the edge. At an inward point, particular care must be taken to control the stitches, because you must resist the tendency to slant the needle, thereby gradually slanting the line of stitching.

End the thread by taking a small holding stitch over the last loop and running the thread under a completed area on the back. When you are running out of thread, it is possible to add a new one invisibly. Before you end off your old thread, lay it aside for the time being. Begin a second thread and come up as if you were beginning again, leaving a space wide enough for one stitch. When you have worked a few stitches, put down the new thread, and finish off the old thread. Pass the old thread under the first stitch worked with the new thread, making a stitch in the area where you left a space.

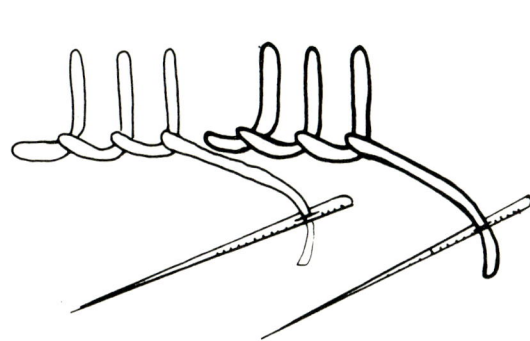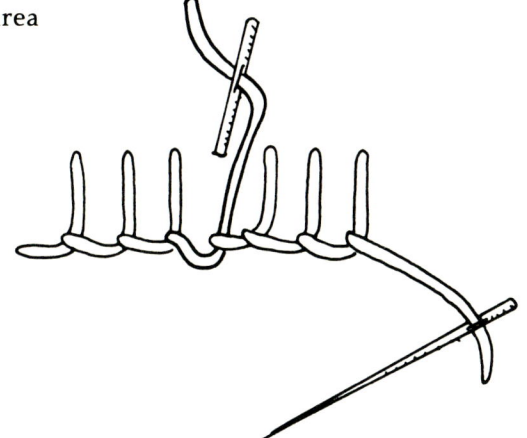

When you pull this into place, the joining will be invisible. Finally, trim away the fabric close to the buttonholed edge.

Couched Braid

Designs for novelty braid work were found among the patterns collected by Virginia Baskervill. These designs were developed by sewing the braid to linen, lawn, piqué, silk, or cashmere. The trim could be applied in many ways. It could be couched down or invisibly tacked in place. Some of the braids used were soutache, rickrack, military, and coronation. Coronation braid is also referred to as coronation cord. This trim, seldom seen today, is a firmly woven cord which is alternately thick and thin. The core is made of cotton, and the outer surface is wrapped with a highly mercerized cotton which has a shiny appearance.

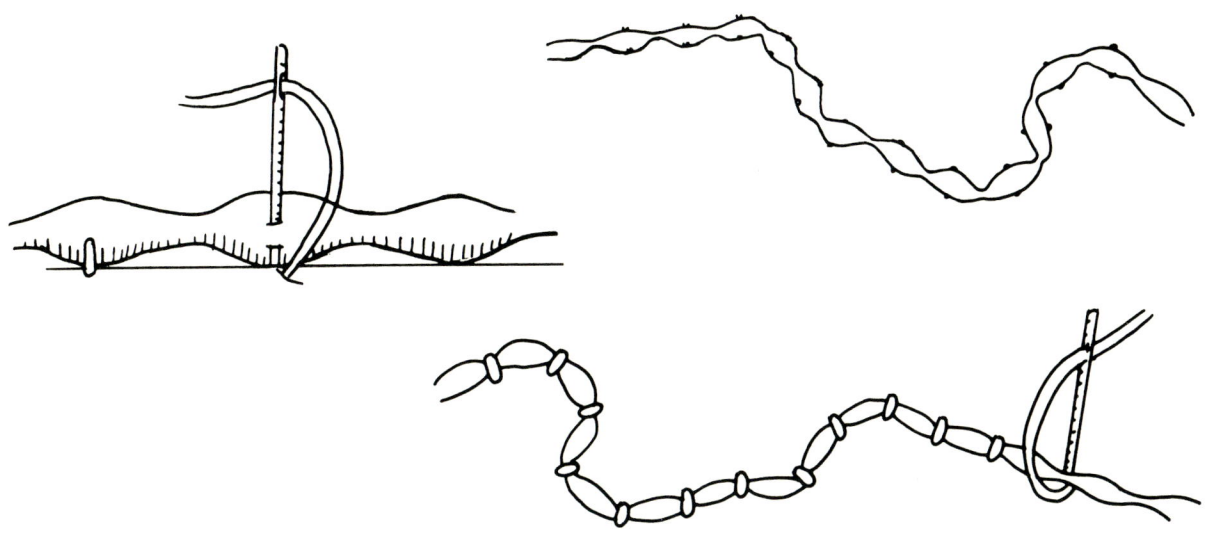

231

Detached Buttonhole

Detached buttonhole is also called needlelace. It is used to make laces which stand alone, and it is often found as a filling for an open area of embroidery. It is made up of buttonhole stitches worked without going into the fabric except at the edges. There are many, many variations of the basic stitch which is shown here. Consult one of the lace books in the bibliography for more information.

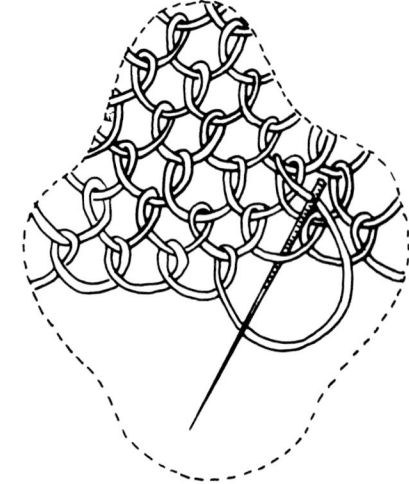

Dot Stitch

Although shown in some embroidery manuals as two stitches, side-by-side, a variation of the dot stitch is often a feature of commercial whitework. It may be done quickly and effectively. To work this stitch, take five or six stitches through the same hole. The completed stitch looks like a tiny, padded satin stitch in a somewhat oval shape. Arrange five of these around a center dot to make a small flower.

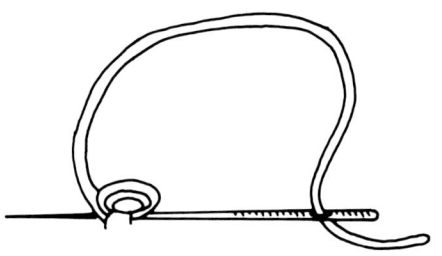

Eyelets

Eyelets can be done single or in rows and can be used in a variety of shapes. Broderie anglaise uses only eyelets to make up floral and geometric designs. First work a row of running stitch around the shape.

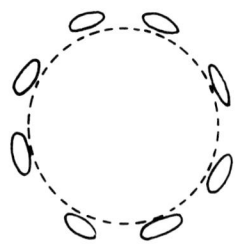

Next work a second row in which all the spaces of the first row are filled. These running stitches are essential to maintaining the size and shape of the eyelet as it is completed.

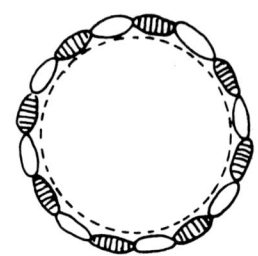

Eyelet holes less than 3/16 inch in diameter may be opened with a pointed tool called a stiletto. Insert the point of the stiletto into the center of the shape, and gently push the thread back to the running stitch line.

If the eyelet hole is larger than 3/16 inch in diameter, cut an x in the center, being careful not to cut the running stitches. Do not remove any fabric.

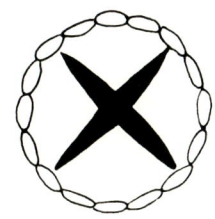

Fold the flaps of fabric back under the work while you overcast when you are working a pierced eyelet. Any excess may be trimmed away when the stitching is complete. Come up in the fabric and down into the hole. When the eyelet is completed, insert the stiletto from the back to lift the stitches toward the front of the work.

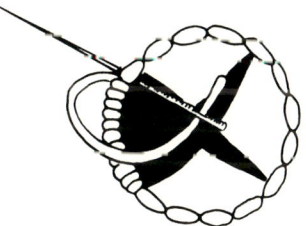

French and Eyelet Stitch

French and eyelet stitch is a combination of padded satin and eyelet stitches.

When working a line of eyelets which touch each other, stitch the running stitch foundation in a serpentine fashion, working over the first hole and under the next, turning at the final hole and coming back. The overcasting of the holes is done in the same serpentine fashion as the running stitch foundation.

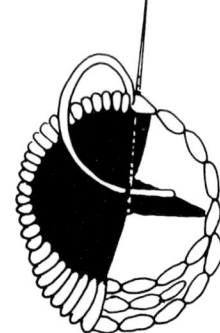

Padding may be added to one side of an eyelet, as shown in these diagrams. Heavily padded eyelets stitched in this manner offer a play of light and shadow which gives great dimension to the embroidery. Rows of padded eyelets are worked in the same manner as rows of regular eyelets.

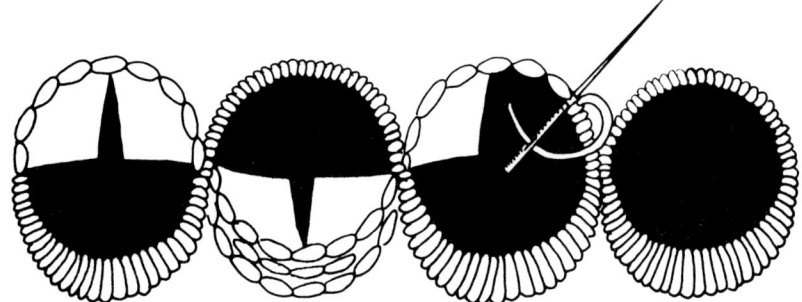

Hedebo Buttonhole

Hedebo embroidery takes its name from Hedebo, in Denmark. It is used to fill open areas, creating a floral or geometric pattern.

The design is drawn on medium-weight linen. Then the stitching is worked, and the fabric is cut away from behind the worked areas. The stitching sequence is similar to that of simple cutwork. First a row of double running stitch is worked around a shape. (See eyelet stitch.) Next a row of knotted buttonhole stitch is worked, going from left to right.

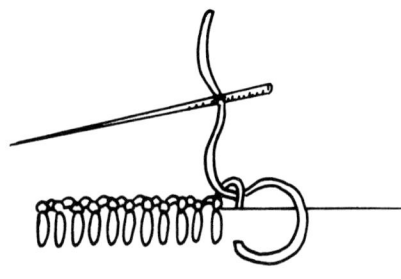

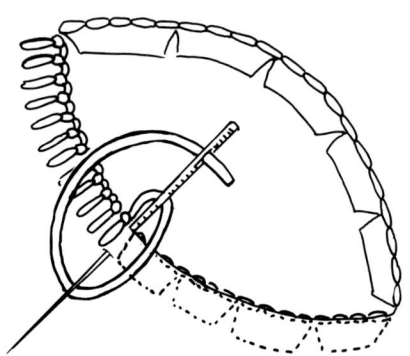

When the stitches reach the end of a bar which is to cross an open space, threads are laid across, back, and across, then the Hedebo buttonhole stitch is worked on the bar back to the first point of departure.

Often small rings are stitched separately and incorporated in the filling of large open spaces. To aid in making these uniformly, a Hedebo ring stitch is used. This is a graduated stick of turned wood or clear plastic. The thread is wrapped around the stitch, and the Hedebo buttonhole stitch is worked over it, using the same thread. When the ring is completed, the thread is left attached and is used to connect the ring to the other stitching.

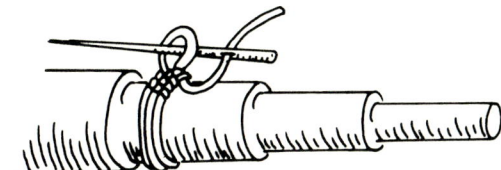

Mountmellick Stitch

Mountmellick embroidery incorporates a wide variety of stitches. It is most often worked on satin jean, a cotton fabric with a thick, soft cotton thread. Traditional uses were for table and bed linens. It is helpful to imagine a triangle which lies on top of the design line when working this stitch. Begin by coming up at A, down at B, and out again at C for Step 1.

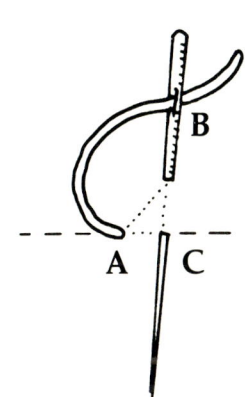

Step 1

Step 2 is accomplished by passing the needle under the stitch created in Step 1.

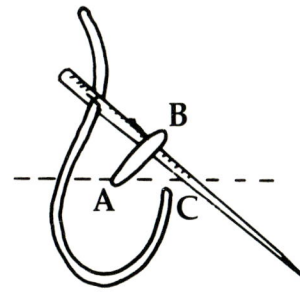

Step 2

The needle goes down at A and up at C, with the thread held behind the tip of the needle, for Step 3.

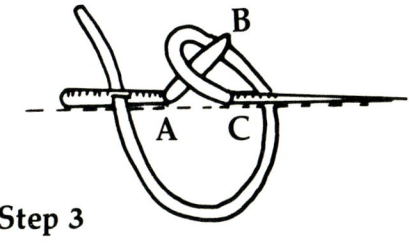

Step 3

As you go to the next stitch, imagine another triangle.

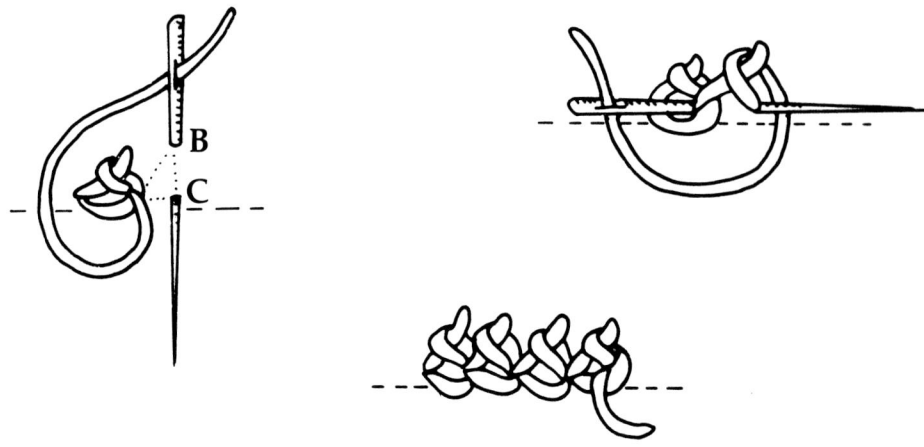

Overcast Edges

Overcast edges are an alternative to buttonhole edges. Threads are trailed along the line which is to be the edge of the article (see Trailing) and covered with closely spaced stitches. Often a large bundle of threads is used, giving a very heavy edge.

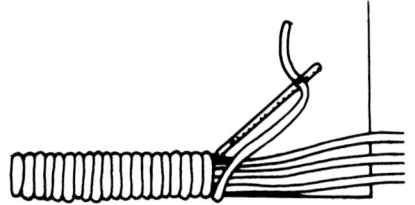

Padded Satin Stitch

This is perhaps the stitch which most often comes to mind when the term whitework is mentioned. It is used in many of the nineteenth- and early twentieth-century types.

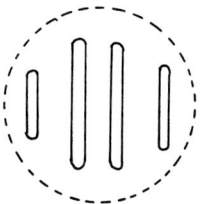

This stitch can be used in almost any shape. The size of the motif is a consideration, since stitches which are more than 1/2 inch long may tend to separate or be otherwise difficult to control. Large shapes are often subdivided and embroidered in sections to avoid this problem. In most shapes the surface stitches lie perfectly parallel, but some fanning can be done in shapes which bend. It is important to keep in mind that harder threads, such as coton à broder, do not fan well.

To begin padded satin stitch, first work a layer of satin stitch within the final outline of your shape. This is done in the surface satin manner, that is, going down and coming up on the same side of the shape, leaving only a row of tiny stitches around the shape on the reverse side. Padded satin stitch can be worked in high or low relief. Experiment to see how many layers of padding you will need for the thread you are using. If you are using more than one layer of padding, be sure to leave enough space so that each successive layer can be slightly larger than the previous one, yet still be within the outline.

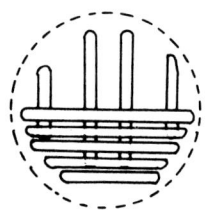

Alternate directions for each layer of padding, but be sure the thread in the last layer is worked at a right angle to the final surface stitching. Plan carefully, so that your last layer will be in the correct direction. Work the final layer in satin stitch, covering the back side of the work as well as the front. When this stitch is worked in a rounded shape, it is generally easier to begin in the center, working first to one side and then to the other. Although the padding is usually done with the same thread as the final layer, some embroiderers prefer to use cotton, a firmer and less expensive thread, under silk thread.

Parma Stitch

Parma stitch creates a large, bold effect, and is a wonderful technique for table linens, bed linens, and articles which are often washed. There are many stitches in Parma embroidery, but the one which is most typical, Parma stitch, is shown here. For more detail, see the books in the bibliography.

Begin by stitching three parallel rows of equally sized chain stitches, following the line of the design.

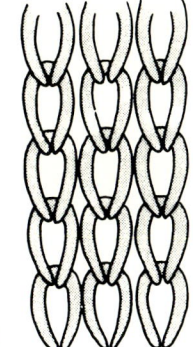

Step 1

The stitch is completed by working two rows of detached buttonhole stitch, using the rows of chain stitch done in the first step as a foundation.

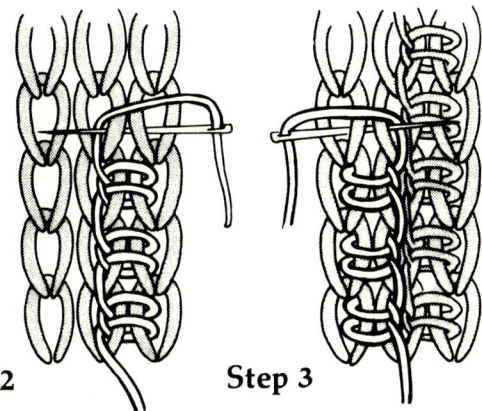

Step 2   **Step 3**

Point de Paris

Point de Paris, also called pin stitch, is a decorative embroidery stitch which is used for holding hems in place, for attaching lace, and in fabric appliqué. The stitch is composed of two parts. The thread is pulled quite firmly while doing the first part of the stitch to open a line of holes at the edge of the fabric or trim being applied. These stitches should be about 1/16 inch long.

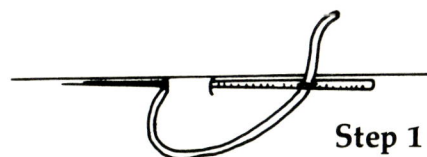

Step 1

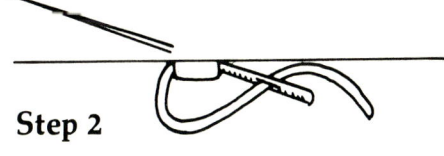

Step 2

Point de Paris is often used to apply insertion lace to fabric. The fabric behind the lace may be trimmed away close to the line of stitches, since each stitch is so small and pulled so tightly.

Step 3

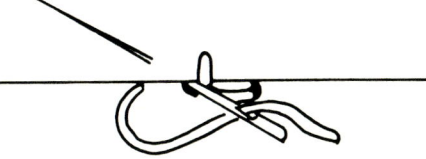

Punch Work

Punch work is often used for stitching fillings in floral motifs. For large areas, sheets of iron-on dots were available. The method of working resembled that of pulled thread patterns such as the four-sided stitch or three-sided stitch, except that the holes were created rather than pre-existed in an even-weave fabric. The punch needle, shown here, is no longer made. The enlarged mid-section of the needle shaft helped to open a hole of sufficient and uniform size.

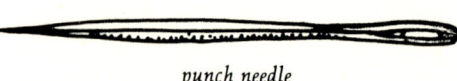

punch needle

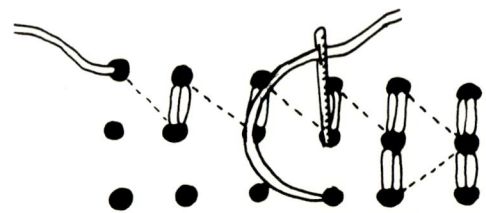

Shadow Work

Traditionally, shadow work has been done from the back side of the ground fabric, using herringbone stitch. An alternative method is to do the stitch from the front side of the fabric, using double backstitch. Begin and end your thread with great care, making sure to do so only on the design line, where it will be hidden by later stitching. The diagrams show the order in which stitches are done in negotiating various types of shapes.

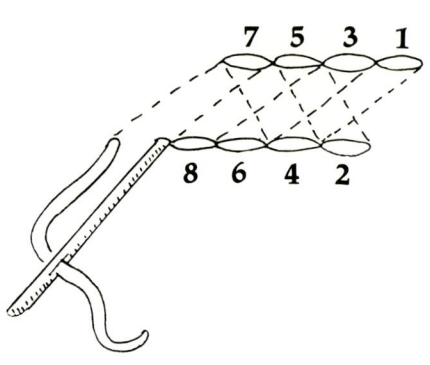

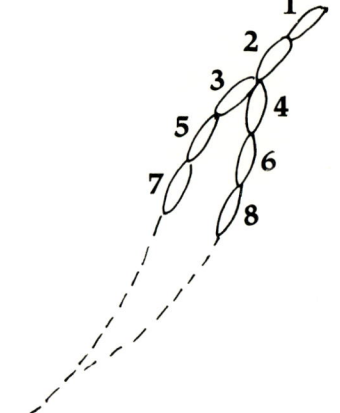

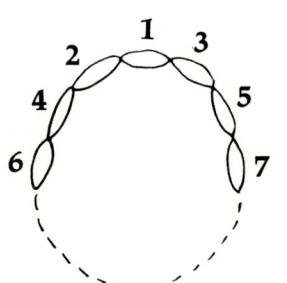

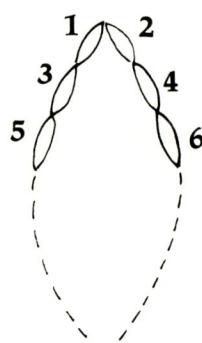

Tambour Work

Tambour work is traditionally worked on a fairly fine fabric which has been stretched on a hoop. The resemblance of this arrangement to a drum head has given rise to its name, tambour, from the French for drum. A tambour hook resembles a crochet hook. It is held upright, so that the hook goes straight down into the fabric. The thread unwinds from a ball held beneath the hoop in the left hand, and tension is kept on the thread as it is pulled to the surface. The stitch is often mistaken for chain stitch.

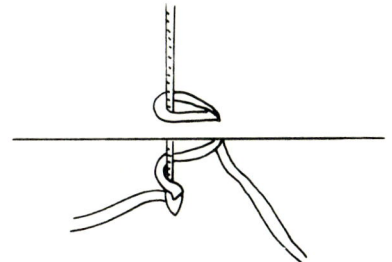

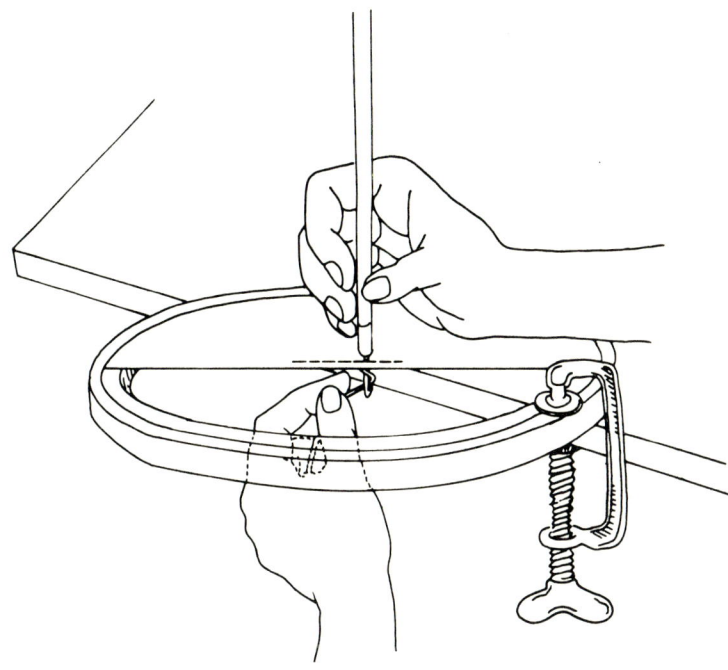

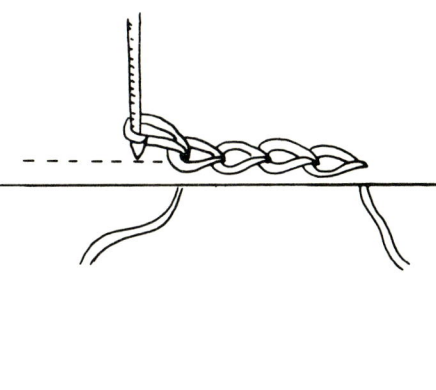

Tape Lace

Tape lace, sometimes called Battenberg lace, employs a machine-made tape foundation. First the tape is basted to a pattern, easing the curves as the tape is laid. Some tapes have a thread woven into the side which may be pulled to gather the tape. With other tapes it is necessary to whip along the edge to gather it. A fairly coarse cotton is used to work filling stitches. Simple laces may employ only herringbone (Russian) stitch, but more complex executions employ a wide variety of detached buttonhole stitch fillings, creating lighter or denser fillings.

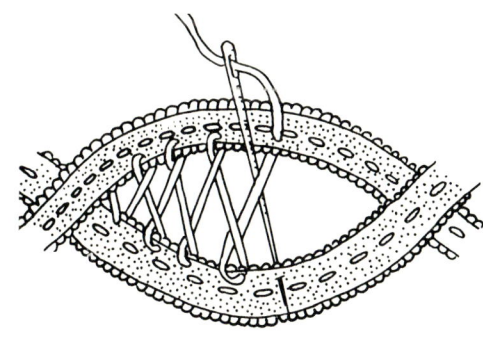

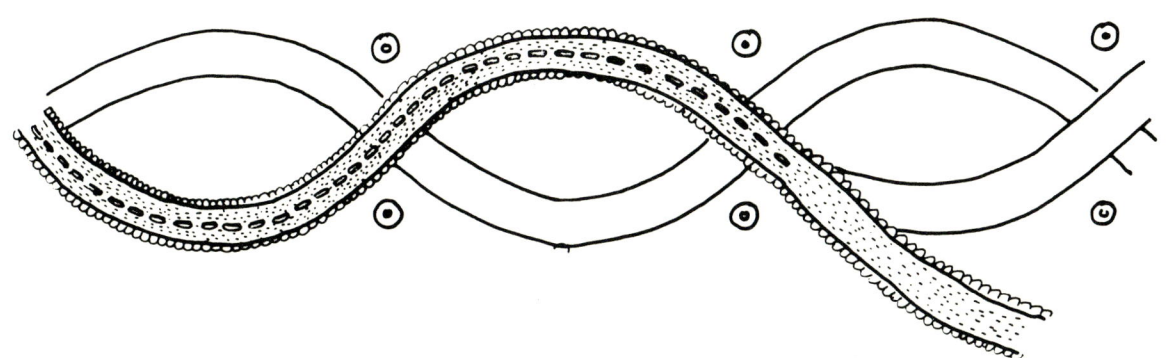

Trailing

Trailing is used for fine lines of stitching. It is the tiniest linear stitch that still has dimension and many have found that it lends itself well to monogramming.

Anchor one or more strands of thread at the end of the line to be worked to serve as padding. This can be done with an away waste knot, as the thread will simply be cut flush with the back of the work after the final stitching is done. The padding thread can be the same that is used for the final stitching, or something firmer.

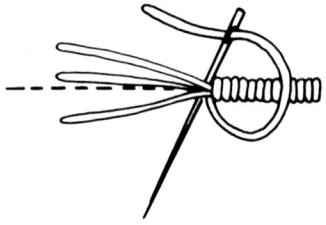

Work tiny satin stitches over the padding thread with a single strand of embroidery thread. Slant the needle up from under the center of the padding thread, and go down on the far side, again slanting the needle. The goal is to hide the needle holes under the padding thread. Keep tension on the padding thread to prevent wobbling of the stitched line.

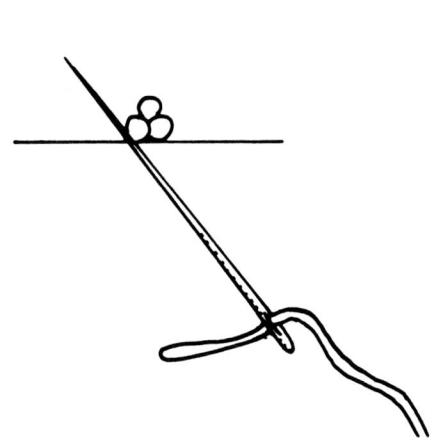

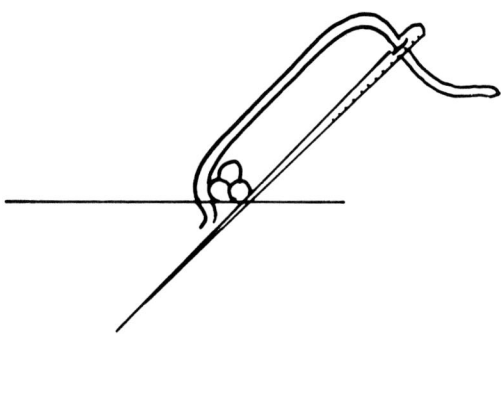

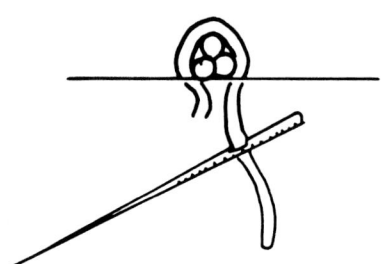

Bibliography

Anchor Manual of Needlework. Newton Centre, MA: Charles T. Branford, 1974.

Bath, Virginia Churchill. *Lace.* New York: Penguin Books, 1979.

Caulfeild, Sophia Frances Anne and Blanche Saward. *Encyclopedia of Victorian Needlework.* New York: Dover, 1972.

Christie, Mrs. Archibald. *Samplers and Stitches.* London: Batsford, 1950.

Dawson, Barbara. *Whitework Embroidery.* London: Batsford, 1987.

de Dillmont, Therese. *Encyclopedia of Needlework.* Mulhouse, France: D. M. C., 1971.

Earnshaw, Pat. *Lace in Fashion.* London: Batsford, 1985.
—*The Identification of Lace.* England: Shire Publications, 1980.

Enthoven, Jacqueline. *The Stitches of Creative Embroidery.* New York: Van Nostrand Reinhold, 1964.

Fry, Gladys Windsor. *Embroidery and Needlework.* London: Pitman, 1950.

Mani di Fata Encyclopedia of Needlework. Milan: Case Editrice Mani di Fata, no date. (in Italian)

Minter, David C. *Modern Needlecraft.* London: Blackie and Son, 1932.

Morris, Barbara. *Victorian Embroidery.* New York: Universe Books, 1970.

Petersen, Grete. *Stitches and Decorative Seams.* New York: Van Nostrand Reinhold, 1983.

Petersen, Grete and Else Svennås. *Handbook of Stitches.* New York: Van Nostrand Reinhold, 1970.

Picken, Mary Brooks. *Language of Fashion: Dictionary and Digest of Fabric, Sewing, and Dress.* New York: Mary Brooks Picken School, Inc., 1939.

Rast, Betty. *Basic Embroidery.* Primer Series. Birmingham, AL: Belles and Beaus, nd.
—*Basic Embroidery II.* Primer Series. Birmingham, AL: Belles and Beaus.
—*Broderie Anglaise.* Primer Series. Birmingham, AL: Belles and Beaus.
—*Shadow Work.* Primer Series. Birmingham, AL: Belles and Beaus.

Scoular, Marion. *Satin Stitch and Trailing.* San Diego: ASN Publishing, 1989.
—*Shadow Embroidery.* San Diego: ASN Publishing, 1989.

Simeon, Margaret. *The History of Lace.* London: Stainer and Bell, 1979.

Van Wyk, Hetsie. *Embroider Now.* Johannesburg, South Africa: Perskor, 1977.

Walker, Carolyn and Kathy Holman. *The Embroidery of Madiera.* New York: Union Square Press, 1987.

Wardle, Patricia. *Victorian Lace.* Bedford, England: Ruth Bean, 1982.

Weldon's Editors. *Encyclopedia of Needlework.* London: Weldon's, Ltd., circa 1930.

Wilson, Erica. *Erica Wilson's Embroidery Book.* New York: Scribner, 1973.

Sources for Supplies

American Crewel and Canvas Studio
P.O. Box 453
Canastota, NY 13032

Bear Threads
4651 Roswell Road, Suite D-308
Atlanta, GA 30342

Eugene Chernin
1401 Germantown Avenue
Philadelphia, PA 19122

Dunwoody's Needle Accent
5477 Chamblee-Dunwoody Road
Dunwoody, GA 30338

The Embroidery Stop
1042 Victory Drive
Yardley, MA 19067

Garden Fairies Trading Company
685 Clover Drive
Santa Rosa, CA 95401

Lacis
3163 Adeline Street
Berkeley, CA 94703

Needle Arts, Inc.
2211 Monroe
Dearborn, MI 48124

Thread Needle Street
35 West Sunset Way
Issaquah, WA 98027

Joan Toggitt, Ltd.
35 Fairfield Place
West Caldwell, NJ 07006

Wichelt Imports, Inc.
Rural Route 1
Stoddard, WI 54658